The Global Beauty Industry

The Global Beauty Industry: Colorism, Racism, and the National Body is an interdisciplinary text that uses beauty to explore topics of gender, race, class, colorism, nation, bodies, multiculturalism, transnationalism, and intersectionality. Integrating materials from a wide range of cultural and geopolitical contexts, it coalesces with initiatives to produce more internationally relevant curricula in fields such as sociology, as well as cultural, women's/gender, media, and globalization studies.

Meeta Rani Jha is a feminist sociologist and an anti-racist activist. She is a scholar-in-residence at Beatrice Bain Research Group (BBRG) in the Gender and Women's Studies Department at the University of California, Berkeley, US. She has taught sociology, globalization, transnational feminist cultural studies, critical race, ethnicity, and media studies at a number of universities in the San Francisco Bay area (currently at the University of San Francisco, US) and in London. For a long time she was a community organizer on issues of racial discrimination, low pay, migration, domestic violence, and homeworking in the UK.

Framing 21st Century Social Issues

Series Editor: France Winddance Twine, University of California–Santa Barbara, USA

The goal of this new, unique series is to offer readable, teachable "thinking frames" on today's social problems and social issues by leading scholars. These are available for view on http://routledge. customgateway.com/routledge-social-issues.html.

For instructors teaching a wide range of courses in the social sciences, the Routledge *Social Issues Collection* now offers the best of both worlds: originally written short texts that provide "overviews" to important social issues *as well as* teachable excerpts from larger works previously published by Routledge and other presses.

As an instructor, click to the website to view the library and decide how to build your custom anthology and which thinking frames to assign. Students can choose to receive the assigned materials in print and/or electronic formats at an affordable price.

Available

The Global Beauty Industry
Colorism, Racism, and the National Body
Meeta Rani Jha

Oversharing, Second Edition
Presentations of Self in the Internet Age
Ben Agger

Social Problems
A Human Rights Perspective
Eric Bonds

The Enduring Color Line in U.S. Athletics
Krystal Beamon and Chris M. Messer

Identity Problems in the Facebook Era
Daniel Trottier

The Pains of Mass Imprisonment
Benjamin Fleury-Steiner and Jamie G. Longazel

From Trafficking to Terror
Constructing a Global Social Problem
Pardis Mahdavi

Unequal Prospects
Is Working Longer the Answer?
Tay McNamara and John Williamson

Beyond the Prison Industrial Complex
Crime and Incarceration in the 21st Century
Kevin Wehr and Elyshia Aseltine

Girls With Guns
Firearms, Feminism, and Militarism
France Winddance Twine

Terror
Social, Political, and Economic Perspectives
Mark P. Worrell

Torture
A Sociology of Violence and Human Rights
Lisa Hajjar

DIY
The Search for Control and Self-Reliance in the 21st Century
Kevin Wehr

The Global Beauty Industry
Colorism, Racism, and the National Body

Meeta Rani Jha

Routledge
Taylor & Francis Group

LONDON AND NEW YORK

First published 2016
by Routledge
711 Third Avenue, New York, NY 10017

and by Routledge
2 Park Square, Milton Park, Abingdon, Oxon, OX14 4RN

Routledge is an imprint of the Taylor & Francis Group, an informa business

Library of Congress Cataloging in Publication Data
Jha, Meeta Rani.
The global beauty industry : colorism, racism, and the national body/
by Meeta Rani Jha.
    pages cm. – (Framing 21st century social issues)
Includes bibliographical references and index.
1. Beauty contests. 2. Beauty, Personal–Social aspects. 3. Beauty
culture–Social aspects. 4. Sex role. 5. Women–Identity. 6. Racism.
7. Nationalism. I. Title.
HQ1219.J495 2016
646.7'2–dc23   2015011689

ISBN: 978-1-138-18841-9 (hbk)
ISBN: 978-1-138-83943-4 (pbk)
ISBN: 978-1-315-73343-2 (ebk)

Typeset in Adobe Garamond
by Sunrise Setting Ltd, Paignton, UK

MIX
Paper from
responsible sources
FSC FSC® C013056
www.fsc.org

Printed and bound in Great Britain by
TJ International Ltd, Padstow, Cornwall

Contents

~~~

Series Foreword

The first decades of the twenty-first century have been a time of paradoxes. Growing prosperity and the growth of the middle classes in countries such as Brazil, China, India, Russia, and South Africa have been accompanied by climate change, environmental degradation, labor exploitation, sexual abuse and sexual violence targeting girls and women, state censorship of social media, governmental corruption, and human-rights abuses. Sociologists offer theories, concepts, and analytical frames that enable us to better understand the challenges and cultural transformations of the twenty-first century. How can we generate new forms of collective knowledge that can help solve some of our local, global, and transnational problems?

We live in a world in which new communication technologies and products such as mobile cellular phones, iPads, and new social media such as Facebook, Google, Skype, and Twitter have transformed online education, global communication networks, and local and transnational economies; facilitated revolutions such as the 'Arab Spring'; and generated new forms of entertainment, employment, protest, and pleasure. These social media have been utilized by social-justice activists, political dissidents, educators, entrepreneurs, and multinational corporations. They have also been a resource employed to facilitate corporate deviance, government corruption, and the increased surveillance of civilian populations. This form of use threatens democracy, privacy, creative expression, and political freedoms.

This is the fifth year of our Routledge 'Framing 21st Century Social Issues' series. Our series includes books on topics ranging broadly from climate change, consumption, eugenics, torture, sports, medical technologies, gun violence, the internet, and youth culture. These books explore contemporary social problems in ways that introduce basic sociological concepts in the social sciences, cover key literature in the field, and offer original diagnoses. They also engage directly in current debates within the social sciences over how to best define, rethink, and respond to the social concerns that preoccupy the early twenty-first century.

The goal of this series is to provide accessible essays that examine a wide range of social issues with local, global, and transnational impact. Sociologists are ideally poised to contribute to a global conversation about a range of issues such as the impact of mass incarceration on local economies, medical technologies, health disparities, violence, torture, transnational migration, militarism, and the AIDS epidemic. The contributors to this series bring the works of classical sociology into dialogue with contemporary social theorists from diverse theoretical traditions including but not limited to feminist, Marxist, and European social theory.

Readers do not need an extensive background in academic sociology to benefit from these books. Each book is student friendly in that we provide glossaries of terms for the uninitiated that are keyed to bolded terms in the text. Each chapter ends with questions for further thought and discussion. The books are ideal for undergraduates because they are accessible without sacrificing a theoretically sophisticated and innovative analysis.

Meeta Rani Jha provides a unique analysis of the global beauty industry. Moving between the US, India, and China, Jha provides an intersectional analysis that illuminates how class, caste, colorism, and nationalism structure how beauty is defined at the local, national, and global level. Beauty is a site of struggle over class, caste inequality, racism, and respectability. For example, in the US, darker skin tones have been racialized, stigmatized, and correlated with lower wages, lower-status spouses, lower levels of education, and restricted social mobility. For US blacks, the negative relationship between skin color and social mobility has been well documented. In other words, beauty—which is partially defined by skin color—is a resource. The political economy and cultural politics of beauty is an important topic for those interested in the ways that beauty hierarchies are intertwined with racism, class, ethnic inequalities, and the socio-political consequences of global capitalism. This book will inspire the reader to think more critically about skin color, class, and the body, and beauty as a form of embodied capital. In a capitalist economy in which beauty can provide access to higher-income spouses, higher education, and more financial security, women and (increasingly) men are willing to go to great lengths to alter their skin color, hair color, and other features as they participate in a global consumer economy. This book is ideal for courses on gender, cultural sociology, sociology of the body, and global studies.

France Winddance Twine
Series Editor

Preface

This book introduces readers to a nuanced analysis of beauty, starting with US culture and then taking a global and transnational perspective. Its aim is to introduce beauty as an analytical category to examine the intersectionality of gender relations. Beauty cultures are formed and reproduced in a political context of globalization, colonialism, and capitalism, and often illuminate local societal conflicts. The concept of "beauty capitalism" best describes the importance of consumption to the different institutions using beauty, sexuality, and femininity as a marketing device in Western-dominated media and transnational consumer culture. The commodification of women's bodies constitutes the marketing and brand logic of capitalism, and the exploitation of migrant and Third World women's labor drives its profit and expansion. The book opens up feminist theories pertaining to beauty and femininity that explain the ways in which beauty standards are used to regulate women's bodies and lives, highlighting the role of mediated beauty pageants in gendered nationalism and consumer cultures in three different national contexts: the US, India, and China. I examine the ways in which a global Eurocentric beauty aesthetic takes different forms and is given value in different ways in Indian and Chinese national contexts because of differing colonial and semi-colonial national histories and geopolitics.

Each chapter integrates the larger framing questions of how we can use beauty analytically to understand and think about beauty's imbrication in structural power relations of gender, race, nation, class, caste, inequality, and global culture by using an intersectional framework. The case studies of the Miss America pageant and the 1968 second-wave feminist protests, the Black Is Beautiful social movement, black popular and musical cultures and global icons such as Beyoncé, beauty contests, the skin-lightening industry, Bollywood celebrities such as Aishwarya Rai and their cultural influence, beauty protests such as Dark is Beautiful and Brown n' Proud in India, and the beauty contests and cosmetic industry in China provide a richly textured analysis of beauty by opening up complex theoretical debates on feminisms, nationalism, colonialism, racism, internalized racism, casteism, internal migration and inequality, cultural and media globalization, diaspora, and transnationality.

Acknowledgments

I would not have written this book without the generosity, kind encouragement, and guidance of France Winddance Twine. A chance meeting and a discussion on beauty, racism, and colorism in New York at the American Sociology Conference 2013 eventually resulted in a book proposal.

I am indebted to feminist activists, filmmakers, and scholars who have opened up the analysis of multiple dimensions of beauty, allowing me to build on their work and produce this book. I am also very grateful to three anonymous reviewers who gave valuable feedback in the conception of the book and in the development of the first two chapters.

I am fortunate to have the love of many people in my life: of my parents—my mother, Pratibha Jha, and my father, Dr Ganesh Dutt Jha—of my siblings, and of alternative families in Manchester, London, Berkeley, and San Francisco. In particular, I would like to acknowledge Neeta Jha and Lynne Humphrey for their unwavering presence and nurture in my life. Thanks to John Landahl, whose love of learning motivates my reading, and to Tinku (Ali) Istiaq for mulling over the cover for this book. I am grateful for the many beautiful people in my life, whose energy keeps my heart warm and my mind seeking better understanding.

Introduction

On September 15, 2013 Nina Davuluri was crowned Miss America 2014 (Figure I.1), generating publicity and racial controversy in the US. She was disparaged as "un-American," as a "terrorist," "Muslim," and as an "Arab." Her win at a particular historical moment articulated the expression of anti-Muslim racism and Islamophobia that has become a national and global norm since 9/11. Only nine women of color have won the pageant since its inception in 1921, and Miss Davuluri (a South Asian born in New York whose parents migrated from South India) is the first woman of South Asian ancestry to be crowned as Miss America. What meanings are created about US national identity when an Indian (South Asian) American is crowned as the queen of beauty?

To be crowned as the most beautiful woman in the US is the ultimate **American dream** for many young American women and girls. Beauty pageants such as this are national media events, a site of **gendered socialization** in so far as they promote gendered norms of beauty that shape cultural ideas of femininity. Girls of color have watched Disney fairy tales from a young age—most often seeing the blond, blue-eyed, white princess being rescued by a handsome prince and living happily ever after—and now a young woman with dark skin like theirs has been crowned queen! Eurocentric beauty ideals, valorized in beauty pageants and Disney films, exercise social control over female bodies generating fantasies, inspiration, injury, and inequality. Women can attain or approximate this beauty ideal only if they can mold, sculpt, manipulate, and reshape their body according to culturally validated norms. The fantasy of **patriarchal** heterosexual bliss of the white princess is conveyed as the feminine equivalent of the American dream, achievable through consumer practices of grooming, hygiene, fashion, fitness, hair and skin care, and surgical modification, simultaneously producing racism, sexism, heterosexism, and classism in everyday media practices.

The rise in the number of women undergoing cosmetic surgery to "improve" and "transform" themselves has been declared as a gendered psychological and physical health epidemic by feminists such as Naomi Wolf (1991), Sandra Bartky (1990), Susan Bordo (2003) and Peg Brand (2000). These feminists have made us aware how beauty companies have created an entire range of inadequacies and beauty-related pathologies that enact a new form of social control on women's lives through beauty

Figure I.1 Nina Davuluri, Miss America 2014 winner

Source: Donald Kravitz/Getty Images.

rituals. Moral judgments inscribed in images of bodies not fitting into conventional beauty and slim ideals create stigma.

Susan Bordo (2003:16) explains that body is not only an individual material asset but also a site of cultural and political struggles. Women's bodies are a battleground fought over by religious ideologies and national and political institutions as well as by media, beauty, and health corporations. The cultural norms of a society inscribe meanings in order to socialize and discipline female bodies, which Bordo points out are socially regulated and molded by patriarchy and **capitalism** as well as by feminist resistance.

Beauty markets are primarily based on production and consumption of feminine beauty, sexuality, and youthfulness. The commodification of women's bodies, in accentuating their sexual differences, has generated "sexiness" as an imperative for women. Beauty and sexuality are constructed as essential and natural attributes of femininity and female identity. Consumption offers women the means to commodify and consume femininity to gain status, validation, and identity. As Celia Lury (1996) and Don Slater (1997) remind us, consumer practices are an integral aspect of modern experience and inscribe multiple meanings to our bodies, it is important to remember that the rituals of consumption entail not only the trivial and mundane aspects of fulfilling our basic needs, but also the enjoyment and pleasures of fulfilling our deeper desires and wants.

Media representations of femininity and beauty, such as those deployed by the Miss America pageant, can shape identities at the personal, national, and global levels. Beauty works at many levels and has multiple meanings. On an individual level, beauty is a site of subject formation creating identification, dis-identification, and ambivalence. On a national level, women's bodies are read as a metaphor for the national and social body and understood in terms of modernity and traditions. The civilizational status of a country is ranked as developing, developed, backward, or progressive, depending on its levels of Westernization. Hollywood and Disney films, as well as toys such as Barbie dolls, reinforce Eurocentric ideals of beauty all over the world as US consumer capitalism is adopted as an economic model to a greater or lesser degree by most countries in Asia, South America and Africa. We will analyze how three different societies, the US, India, and China, with very different histories and geopolitical contexts, understand and reproduce female bodies, femininity, and beauty in the context of global capitalism and **transnational consumer culture**.

Feminists have challenged beauty pageants because beauty pageants, while masquerading as entertainment and popular culture, mask harmful and restrictive gendered norms that pressure girls and women into accepting unattainable beauty ideals of slimness and physical perfection, causing them physical and psychological harm. Feminists have theorized that beauty plays a key role in the exercise of power and feminine identifications in **contemporary consumer culture**. Naomi Wolf's (1991) *The Beauty Myth* analyzes beauty ideals as a "gold standard" that organizes women into a beauty hierarchy and competition, and takes away their power to define themselves. Physical appearance and attractiveness is a form of privilege (and a type of currency, or capital), as many feminist sociological, psychological, and media-based studies have shown time and time again; it is an upward route to class and economic mobility through better employment options and marital choice. Feminine beauty and physical attractiveness are forms of capital which women can increase by investing in beauty products and in grooming and beauty practices. Physical attractiveness, whiteness, and youthfulness have accrued capital just as darker skin color, hair texture, disability, and aging have devalued feminine currency. Beauty is a resource that continues to be part of unearned privileges not only for white Americans with European origins, but also for those who approximate white physiognomy and light-skin ideals, like Vanessa William, who was the first black woman to be crowned Miss America in 1984.

For 60 years, the Miss America beauty pageant promoted Anglo-European beauty norms. Margaret Hunter (2005:57), researching the beauty practices of African American and Mexican American women, argues that beauty capital is inaccessible to many black women and women of color as it continues to be defined primarily by lighter skin color and Anglo-looking faces, bodies, and straight and blond hair. Hunter (2011:145) introduces the term "**racial capital**" and defines it as "a resource drawn from the body that can be related to skin tone, facial features, body shape, etc." She explains that it is because we live in a racist society that racial capital is a source of advantage in how we are perceived as an individual and does not depend on how we define ourselves. Her concept of racial capital is connected to the intersectional relations of racism, sexism, and **colorism** because beauty consumption is a route to feminine identity. This book examines the role beauty plays in creating structural and individual privilege, as well as contributing to discrimination and inequality. Beauty cultures integrate local, transnational, and international characteristics derived from fashion, media, and advertising discourses, which means beauty is a useful analytical tool with which to investigate power relations at the three different levels: the personal, the national, and the global. The book's case studies focus on the skin-lightening industry and cosmetic surgery as two ways women try to transform their physical appearance in order to increase their racial and **beauty capital** and access labor and marriage markets more successfully. In this way they may be able to reduce the effects of sexism, classism, and racism by gaining economic and cultural mobility. Women of color and working-class white women's desire for middle-class white beauty is founded rationally in their desire to surpass racial and working-class penalties.

What can we learn from beauty pageants about the ways that racial, gender, class, and color hierarchies are recycled and reproduced? This book will examine feminist critiques of beauty pageants that began with the protest in 1968 by feminists organized as the **Women's Liberation Movement**, including a critique of gender norms, beauty as an unattainable ideal, and as one that embodies racialized forms of oppression. We will also examine feminist views that argue that beauty is not wholly oppressive and needs to be contextualized in women's local power relations and their experiences of leisure, pleasure, and communal bonding.

Another question that we will consider is whether, as the pageant changes and adapts to new societal norms, the old Eurocentric ideals of beauty are being replaced with new, inclusive, and multicultural ones. Thirty years before Nina Davuluri was crowned Miss America, Vanessa Williams, a light-skinned woman of mixed African ancestry, also faced a racist backlash when, in 1983, she became the first black woman to win the title of Miss America. The "white" ideal of feminine beauty was enshrined by the Miss America pageant at its inception in 1921—an era of racist Jim Crow segregation, when only young white women in good health were allowed to compete (women of color and women with disabilities were prohibited from participating). The mutual constitution of femininity and sexual chastity was meant to assure white purity in a racist society that practiced **eugenicist policies** and anti-**miscegenation** laws. This kind of social control of women's bodies has been a persistent mechanism in creating and maintaining racial and cultural purity. Visible physical characteristics such as skin color (as well as hair texture and nose and lip shape) became markers of social difference, and part of a process of racialization through which the concept of "race" is given specific social meaning. The power of beauty can be understood by examining its racialized and colonial history. Can we interpret the crowning of a woman of South Asian ancestry with dark skin as a sign that the dominant standards of white beauty have been displaced by a more inclusive multicultural, multiracial, and multiethnic beauty standard? Although not all ethnic minorities have dark skin (for example, there are very light-skinned Chinese, Koreans, Japanese, and "white" Hispanics), it may be affirming for Americans to see this as a sign of racial progress and equality, a marker for the success of the Civil Rights Movement for racial equality. From these examples, we can understand the Miss America beauty pageant as a site for a struggle over competing ideas of national belonging. Many race scholars and activists writing on race relations analyzed Miss Davuluri's accomplishment as a win for racial equality, one that represents a success story of hard work by a second-generation immigrant, who, undergoing regimes of training to improve and fashion her body to pass countless tests of **American exceptionalism**, overcame obstacles of ethnic difference and **institutional racism** to win at many levels of local and state competitions.

Eduardo Bonilla-Silva's (2006) research shows how racism functions in contemporary America through a **color-blind racial ideology** that situates racism at the individual level, without looking at the larger social or structural mechanisms (such as **internal colonialism**, national policies of **racial assimilation**, the global expansion of capitalism, and the reinforcement of gendered and racialized inequality) through which racism continues to operate. Bonilla-Silva suggests that racial practices during the Jim Crow era were typically overt and clearly racial, whereas today they tend to be covert, institutional, and appear to be non-racial. He highlights unearned privileges, such as **Roosevelt's The New Deal**, primarily made available to working-class Anglo-Americans, that have helped those accruing **white privilege** to succeed. Since the 1980s, due to the consistent pressure from state-wide and local black and ethnic institutions and networks, the Miss America pageant has changed to include diversity, and therefore many understood Miss Davuluri's win as representing racial and ethnic progress for marginalized groups. In Chapter 1, I will examine the ways in which this message is constructed in simple terms that falsify the reality: America seemingly values multicultural diversity and **individualism**, while the social reality of discrimination and institutionalized oppression remain untouched. This illusion is deployed at the same time as the Miss America Corporation has an army of experts and consultants who promote ideas of America to a global market of investors, tourists, and international students. The distinctive national characteristics of **pluralism** and individualism are a way to brand the American trademark in an easily understood way by selecting specific individuals who are seen to embody these values. The key question structuring this book is: "how are skin color, hair texture, facial features, class privilege, and racial or ethnic identities mapped onto ideas of gender norms of beauty and femininity?" An analysis of beauty is important because beauty can be converted into forms of social, economic, and **symbolic power** that devalue and denigrate some physical features while idealizing and privileging others.

More specifically, beauty functions as a symbolic marker of cultural and moral superiority in a hierarchy of racialized difference assigning goodness, godliness, intelligence, competence, success, and femininity to whiteness.

If we consider the image of the white woman in John Gast's 1872 painting *American Progress* (Figure I.2), which was taken as an allegory for America's **Manifest Destiny**, she is carrying a flag and pointing to the land of westward expansion. We can see how gender and femininity was a central trope in the social construction of whiteness. The attributes of white femininity were borrowed from **Enlightenment philosophers**, who understood beauty as a virtuous and divine attribute of truth and justice. Race was defined as a biological category, and racial differences were understood as reflecting the moral character and intelligence of the different racial groups.

Figure I.2 *American Progress* (1872) by John Gast. Called *Spirit of the Frontier* and widely distributed, the settlers are guided and protected by the goddess-like feminine figure of Columbia, personifying the United States of America, and aided by technology (railways, telegraphs) to drive Native Americans and bison into obscurity. It is important to note, too, that Columbia is bringing the "light" from the east to the "darkened" west

Source: Fotosearch/Getty Images.

The superiority of whiteness was consolidated by speaking of it as a moral and progressive force, and nonwhite people were labeled as less beautiful, even ugly, because of their biological differences and thus defined as less moral and less human. The white standard of beauty created a hierarchy of humanness with Europeans at the top of the racial hierarchy. **Scientific racism** in the sciences of anthropology, biology, and psychology has been used historically and geographically to produce knowledge about the "other" and "different" races in order to establish the superiority of the white race and justify colonial and capitalist exploitation. Ronald Hall notes that

> skin-color ranking is primarily derived from European histories of racism where white skinned people from the United States and Europe are viewed as being at the highest stage of civilization followed by the different shades of skin-colors from Asian and the Middle-Eastern countries that are considered semi-developed. The lowest ranking is attributed to people of darker-skin such as Africans or Australian aborigines who are considered the least civilized, primitive, and barbaric.

(2013:4)

Chapter 2 examines one of the most significant anti-racist challenges to Eurocentric beauty ideals: the new beauty norm of the Black Is Beautiful social movement that transformed American culture and identity. This movement used the Afro hairstyle as a symbol of racial pride, and was instigated and popularized by the Black Power and

Civil Rights movements and awakened a black cultural identity, which was inextricably tied up with decolonizing minds and consciousness. Black leaders, intellectuals, cultural workers, and musicians, challenged Eurocentric knowledge production that characterized Africans and black Americans as subhuman and uncivilized. Blackness was given a new meaning and a new symbolism to reconstruct black pride.

bell hooks, reflecting on the relationship of black beauty and black power (1996:119–32), asks "What impact does white supremacy have on our collective psyches, shaping the nature of everyday life?" She argues that the internalized self-deprecation, misogyny and racism that black women navigate is logical in the context of white supremacy. She highlights the importance of culture as a site of resistance and cites "the oppositional black culture as one of the few locations that has provided a space for the kind of decolonization that makes loving blackness possible." She proposes a black feminist strategy of collective self-love "as a revolutionary intervention that undermines practices of domination. Loving blackness as political resistance transforms our ways of looking and being, and thus creates the conditions necessary for us to move against the forces of domination and death and reclaim black life."

Beauty pageants began as an American cultural event and have been adopted by many countries since the 1950s as a **nation-building** strategy. Spread by Hollywood films, beginning in the 1920s, the idea of beauty pageants gained prominence, especially in the 1930s and 1940s, and was then quickly appropriated by national elites in the era of **decolonization** and nation-building. The elites of the Third World, South America, South East Asia, Africa, and the Caribbean deployed it as a strategy for unifying diverse ethnic communities into **national publics**, as a part of nation-building efforts. Cohen *et al.* (1996) made the first global comparison of beauty pageants from different parts of the world, exploring them as a site of contestation as well as national unification. They argue that each national beauty contest is simultaneously both local and global, but that different ideas of femininity are constructed for local and global audiences; and Balogun's (2012:357) ethnographic research on two Nigerian beauty pageants found that beauty pageants displayed two different kinds of femininity, constructed for different audiences. She found that the Queen Nigeria pageant aimed at reinforcing cultural pride and national unity by including an African cooking competition, signalling the importance of food and domesticity for African culture; and The Most Beautiful Girl in Nigeria pageant promoted a cosmopolitan vision of Nigerian femininity to a global audience by adhering to global beauty standards.

In addition, beauty pageants are primarily transnational commercial networks for the media, entertainment, fashion, and cosmetic industries. The multinational beauty industries target consumers and create local and global markets for beauty products. Beauty pageants have gained currency as a key node in transnational circuits of capitalist economic and cultural exchange. Millions of viewers participate in beauty pageants, in a mass-mediated entertainment and popular-cultural interaction. The old established media sources (such as newspapers, television, radio, and their internet outlets) and new social-media platforms (such as YouTube, Facebook, Twitter, and weblogs) are key nodes for recycling beauty culture, as it gets transformed and molded in **transnational cultural flows** driven by the logic of marketing exchange and profit. Social imaginaries of beauty are influenced by **multinational corporations** and companies to a great extent, although not entirely. Media is the context in which the circulation of texts, images, and commentary shapes our understanding of how local and global beauty cultures are shared. These global cultural circuits spread values, norms, and culture that tend to promote Western ideals of capitalism and **consumerism**. Because of the asymmetrical power of multinationals as compared with local government structures, this often results in assimilation and the disappearance of local cultures, traditions, and identities.

Beauty companies in association with beauty pageants, fashion magazines, and Hollywood, shape emerging, globalized ideals of beauty. The institutionalization of Eurocentric, white beauty norms of skin color, body size, shape, hair texture, physiognomy, and facial features in beauty pageants the world over has spawned a **global beauty industry** devoted to skin lightening, skin-bleaching creams, corrective cosmetic surgery, dieting, and fashion (Glenn, 2009). The beauty industry expanded in the US during a time (early 1900s) of economic prosperity, accelerated industrialization, and urban development. Geoffrey Jones (2008), exploring the globalization of US beauty ideals and practices, examines the ways in which the US-based beauty and hygiene industries, specifically the soap industry after 1945, imposed cultural norms on other countries. The corporations had to take into consideration local cultural norms and pre-existing consumer habits. He explains that since the 1980s they have deployed segmented marketing techniques to adapt marketing to different ethnic groups, with differing needs, in different locations. Despite this differentiation in targeting different populations, he explains that global beauty corporations were successful in imposing a global ideal in "a lack of body odor, white natural teeth, slim figures, paler skins, and rounder eyes."

Following a **postcolonial** and **transnational feminist** framework, both Chapters 3 and 4 investigate how beauty pageants consolidate a global beauty ideal, which exhibits hybridity in some superficial forms (as in the tokenistic 'inclusion' often seen in advertising) and discuss the crucial role of beauty and gendered ideologies in producing and reproducing nations. Beauty pageants are mass-entertainment and media events, situated in global and transnational cultural flows, which often articulate the economic needs of a national community in an effort to harness a global market through media output. The stories of nations as developed and developing, progressive, and democratic can be invented and reinvented in and through beauty pageants as a way of participation in a global capitalist culture. Beauty pageants are promoted by political parties and market forces in an explicit effort to build a unified, national consensus in a multi-ethnic society. Postcolonial and transnational feminists (Mohanty, 1991; Moallem *et al.*, 1999; Grewal, 1999) have argued that beauty pageants are also a key site of gendered **nationalism**, where young women's bodies are a sign that express community and cultural group values as well as national and racial pride. Mimi Nguyen (2011) writing on how beauty is deployed in the services of

American imperialism in the war in Afghanistan, illuminates clearly how feminism can be used as a "civilizing" discourse when combined with a humanitarian ethos of "saving" Afghan women. She analyzes the narratives of a non-profit organization called Beauty Without Borders, which opened a beauty school in Kabul. This organization uses feminist discourses of rescuing Burqa-clad Afghan women (Burqa is a full veil) by "educating" them about beauty techniques in an effort to modernize and liberate them from their "backward" Muslim culture. We can see that beauty discourses are products of ongoing struggles for economic development and mobility, **modernity**, social prestige, and power in a given context.

The Miss America beauty pageant also generates media and public debates in other national, **diasporic media spaces**. Unlike the contrasting coverage in the US, Indian-based media celebrated and valorized Miss Davuluri's win as a sign of the global rise of a modern Indian nation, culturally and economically. At the same time, an alternative, diasporic, and South Asian American feminist media challenged this interpretation, and many, including Miss Davuluri, criticized the prevalence of **skin-color prejudice and discrimination** that continues to traumatize ordinary Indian women. Dr Asha Rangappa (2013), a **diasporic Indian** academic writing in *The Huffington Post* on the Indian beauty myth, compared the racially progressive nature of US **civil society** with Indian culture's prevalent gender discrimination based on skin color. Beauty pageants became very popular in India around 1991, a period of **economic liberalization** as India opened its borders to multinational capital and transnational media. The rise of consumerism in India correlates with the rise of beauty pageants and the growth of the fashion and cosmetic industries. Beauty pageants in India (as in the US) shape ideas of femininity, ideal beauty, and global national identity. Many transnational feminist scholars (Runkle, 2004; Parameswaran, 2005; Osuri, 2008) have argued that Bollywood cinema, television, celebrities, beauty queens, and advertisements have converged in reinforcing British colonial hangovers of an Indian idealization of lighter-skin complexion referred to as **fair-skin status**. In the Indian context, as in many national contexts, skin-color discrimination has a local history. Specifically in India, it is based on class and **caste stratification** that multinational beauty companies such as L'Oreal and Hindustan Lever (that markets lightening creams across Asia) have exploited through the marketing of facial skin-lightening creams, either in forms of skin bleaching or as sun-protection and/or anti-aging creams. I will examine how an idealization of whiteness and its conflation with modern woman has produced an alarming increase in the proliferation and use of skin-lightening products and treatments in India. Skin-color discrimination in the Indian subcontinent predates the arrival of **British colonialism** and imperialism and has origins in the Hindu religious caste system. This chapter examines the key role of beauty pageants in India in normalizing ideas of fair skin as beautiful.

The book examines the global implications of beauty by focusing on key debates of globalization, modernity, nation formation, gender, and skin-color discrimination in

India. Lighter skin in India is associated with education, upper-class status, and success, thus conflating progress with whiteness, modernity, and Westernization. **"Cosmetic whitening"** is a useful term coined by a group of sociologists, Kathy Russell, Midge Wilson, and Ronald Hall (1992), while investigating the impact of Western standards of beauty on cultures across the globe. They explain the term "cosmetic Westernism," or "the internalized ideal held by people around the world that being lighter skinned and more Western looking is better" (Hall, 2013:xiii). Their book helped to popularize the concept of "colorism" referring to "the prejudices and discriminatory practices surrounding skin color differences that occur not only among Black Americans but also among other populations of color such as Latinos and Asians, both in this country and around the world" (Russell-Cole *et al.*, 2013: -xiii).

Bollywood film celebrity Aishwarya Rai, a former Miss World winner and a L'Oreal brand leader, has been called "the most beautiful woman in the world" by the American CBS program *60 Minutes*, and is considered a global multicultural beauty ideal. Margaret Hunter explains how global beauty corporations that primarily value white beauty often deploy a multicultural hybrid aesthetic to "add light-skinned women of color to their advertisements and as spokespersons for their products" (2005:147). She describes this beauty myth with the phrase "illusion of inclusion," and its message for women of color is that their skin-color and bodies are being validated. The new global multicultural, or hybrid, aesthetic, an approximation to white femininity, is also prevalent in Latin America, and can be evinced in many Miss Universe winners from Venezuela and a few from other Latin American countries where the racial legacy of *mestizaje* valorizes whiteness. Eryn Masi de Casanova (2004) explains that in Ecuador, which has only a 5 percent white and a majority *mestizos* (with mixed European, Spanish, and indigenous origins) population, a dark-skinned woman won the Miss Ecuador pageant for the first time only in 1995. Prevalent is a civil discourse of modern citizenship that validates the progress of the nation on the basis of *blanqueamineto*, or the gradual cultural whitening of the population (Wade, 1997). Alexander Edmonds' research (2007) focuses on the popularity of cosmetic surgery in Brazil. He investigates Brazil's legacy of *mesticagem* (similar to *mestizaje*), racial policies of whitening and browning, and the problems of idealization of a multicultural aesthetic imaginary. *Mesticagem* refers to racial mixing of different groups in Brazil, such as Africans, Europeans, and indigenous Indians through marriage, sexual relations, and procreation. This cultural practice promotes a multicultural and racially mixed society which does not promote fixed racial categories. Edmonds notes that the most popular plastic surgeries in Brazil are the "correction of negroid nose" and "buttock implants." He found that his research participants undergoing plastic surgery understood it as beautifying surgery, in that they wanted to look "prettier," and they often blamed their indigenous or African ancestry for features needing correction and improvement. The surgeons he talked to admitted that "nose moved in the direction of Europe, not Africa" (2007:373). He explains that most Brazilians don't identify with race groups (as compared to the US) so cosmetic surgery is not seen an ethical problem because features as defects are not understood in racial terms and there is no stigma in altering one's racial features. He contextualizes the popularity of cosmetic surgery in national racial history and the eugenicist policies of *blanqueamineto* before the 1930s and the politics of racial mixing after the 1950s. He explains that Gilberto Freyre (1956), a sociologist, anthropologist, and historian, successfully attacked prevalent scientific racism by creating a new nationalist image of Brazil as a "rainbow" nation and popularized the vision of "triumphant brownness," but did not displace an earlier ideology of *embranquiamento* or "whitening." Freyre's idealization of hybridity in the racially mixed brown female body is problematized by Edmonds because of the sexualization of racially mixed women for "brownness" and her African buttocks even as her "facial features and hair textures perceived as negra are stigmatized." One of the most common surgical procedures in Brazil is that of buttock implants, in which fat is redistributed from waist to hips and buttocks. Edmonds concluded that plastic surgery provided under public health does democratize beauty for the poor. However, he questions the nationalist and populist racialized beauty myth celebrating hybridity and racial mixing in popular culture that promotes tanning and ritual sun bathing, which superficially glosses over structural inequalities. The multicultural paradise created in Brazil's national discourses is also challenged by France Winddance Twine's empirical (1998) ethnographic research into racial inequalities in Brazil. She disrupts the prevalent myth of racial democracy in Brazil. She argues that there is hierarchy between brown and darker brown skin, and the nationalist discourses of the harmony of racial mixing conceal institutional racial discrimination for Afro-Brazilians. She notes that black social movements, such as Black Is Beautiful, urge all Afro-Brazilians to valorize blackness and to adopt a proud black and negro identity as a strategy for racial equality. It is important to analyze Brazil's racial history in order to understand that the multicultural hybrid aesthetic can be deceptive and often deployed to mask exclusion of minorities.

Chapter 4 examines the widespread cultural acceptance of cosmetic surgery in China. The socialist–capitalist Chinese state's beauty economy promotes individual consumer feminist empowerment as way to help China's economic growth. Cosmetic ethnic surgery, such as double eyelid surgery (**blepharoplasty**), highlights the undesirability of Asian facial features as "not beautiful," and promotes sexism, racism, and Westernism. Chinese women undergoing surgery view it as accumulating the advantages of beauty, class, urbanity, and femininity in order to compete in the labor and marriage markets. Rural women are excluded and disproportionately affected by growing wealth disparities as they migrate, leaving family behind to search for work in the special economic zones situated in larger cities. The state's contemporary socialist–neoliberal feminism ignores the gender exploitation of large groups of marginalized women, specifically regarding low pay and insecure employment in the beauty industry. Hua Wen (2013:236) prompts us to understand the micro and macro politics of economic transformation by highlighting the contextualized beauty experiences of her interviewees in her ethnographic research in Beijing. She proposes the term "agency within" to explain women's choices to undergo cosmetic surgery, "to describe women's ability to act within specific historical circumstances: women are free, but only within structures of history and power and gender subjugation over which they have no control." She understands that cosmetic surgery for her interviewees is "an investment for personal gains." Putting herself in their position, she argues that cosmetic surgery provides a kind of freedom within the circumstances women are situated in and that they are able to "exercise some level of control over their lives, although it is a costly, painful, and even dangerous option… The more physical capital a woman can hold, the more ability she may have to reshape the social, cultural and economic fields around her."

Similarly, Moreno Figueroa and Rivers-Moore (2013:6) argue that to understand ordinary women's experiences of beauty we need to pay serious attention to everyday cultural practices of beauty. They propose that we need to shift older feminist understanding of beauty as wholly oppressive and instead take what Maxine Leeds Craig (2006) calls a more "complicated stance" in her ethnographic research into black women's experiences of beauty in local beauty parlors in the context of the 1960s Black Power and Civil Rights movements. This complicated stance is an **intersectional** approach, taking gender, nation, race, color, ethnicity, sexuality, and class hierarchies into consideration when focusing on women's everyday experiences and practices of beauty. The term intersectionality was coined by the black feminist scholar Kimberlé Crenshaw (1991), who proposed that race, gender, and class hierarchies were interconnected and co-constituted in black women's experiences. Maxine Leeds Craig's (2006:167) intersectional analysis of her research participants proposed that they negotiate a sense of self through their "beauty work" in relation to dominant white beauty standards, but also in relation to the socially and culturally located beauty standards of black middle-class respectability (in hair straightening) much more prevalent at that time. Craig also pointed out the important role black business women and entrepreneurs have played in opening up spaces of consumption and leisure for other black women. She noted that black women were influenced by competing standards of beauty available in their local context and concluded that beauty is a site of oppression, female bonding, and leisure as well as a significant site of anti-racism. Drawing upon these feminist insights, this book takes an intersectional and transnational approach to investigate beauty as a contradictory site of power, pleasure, privilege, and inequality. I draw from interdisciplinary insights and synthesize debates in gender and women's studies, transnational and postcolonial feminisms, global media and cultural studies, black studies/African American studies, and ethnic studies to explain how an analysis of beauty is vital for an analysis of the complicated social power relations that most women are juggling in order to challenge the beauty myths created by the marketing power of the global media corporations. We need this analysis to comprehend the ways in which each one of us is positioned in networks of power relations and to exercise our individual and/or collective agency to counter the harmful beauty discourses that are gaining legitimacy.

I: Beauty as Structural Inequality

Beauty, Feminist Protests, Nationalism, Neoliberal Femininity

The Miss America beauty pageant described in the Introduction generated a public debate, in mainstream newspapers in New York and New Delhi, and on social-media platforms such as Facebook and Twitter, over competing meanings of beauty, femininity, race, and national belonging. We have already seen how beauty pageants become occasions for controversy, protest, and boycotts, given that they are repositories for popular culture, media representations, and (perhaps most importantly) as they become platforms for beauty companies to create new markets (Cohen *et al.*, 1996).

In this chapter, I begin with a historical discussion of the **second-wave feminist** protest of the Women's Liberation Movement, at the Miss America pageant, and provide an overview of different forms of feminist debates on sexism, gendered nationalism, neoliberal capitalism, multiculturalism, and racism related to the issue of beauty. I provide a brief historical context of feminism for understanding the Miss America contest, and then delve into an analysis of the contemporary moment focused on the recent controversy surrounding Miss Davuluri. Exploring feminist theories of beauty, race, and culture may provide a better understanding of how this annual national ritual operates as an institution and national site for the reproduction and maintenance of racialized gender norms that produce idealized versions of beauty and femininity. Second, I will argue that, while beauty is an embodied social privilege for some, for others it remains a site of inequality, oppression, suffering and disadvantage. Finally, I will interrogate the ways in which women's bodies represent a symbolic space of changing nationalist and multicultural meanings that produce an exceptional neoliberal femininity. Drawing on the scholarship of Wendy Brown (2005) and Nicholas Rose (1990), who theorizes that the dominant mode of subject formation in the contemporary moment is structured by market rationality of liberal capitalism, we can understand the ideal national citizen as demonstrating **neoliberal self-governance**. Brown (2005:37) explains that the logic of liberal capitalism organizes the US social sphere where human activity and subjectivity is shaped by an individualized, entrepreneurial, free-market, and profit (cost–benefit)-seeking rationality. This has resulted in a new kind of neoliberal feminine subject. Thus, neoliberal femininity demonstrated by Miss America pageant contestants displays an understanding of gender inequality as an individual problem erasing its structural foundations.

Beauty as Gender Oppression and Radical Feminism

Miss America as Dream Equivalent To—? In this reputedly democratic society, where every little boy supposedly can grow up to be President, what can every little girl hope to grow to be? Miss America. That's where it's at. Real power to control our own lives is restricted to men, while women get patronizing pseudo-power, an ermine cloak and a bunch of flowers; men are judged by their actions, women by appearance.

> (Morgan, 1970:484; also quoted on redstockings.org)

On 7 September 1968, in her efforts to mobilize women to protest the **Miss America Beauty Pageant**, which was to be held in Atlantic City, Robin Morgan, a founding member of the organization New York Radical Women, outlined ten reasons for "No More Miss America," and the quote above was her ninth reason. In 1921, the Miss America pageant began as a beach-side bathing-suits showcase and then evolved into a state and national competition. Since the 1990s it has changed to a **not-for-profit corporation**, which comprises a vast network of local state organizations, volunteers, and financial supporters and has become a scholarship program (Miss America Organization website).

New York Radical Women (NYRW) was founded in 1967 in New York City by Shulamith Firestone, Carol Hanisch, Pam Allen, and Robin Morgan. The Civil Rights Movement served as an inspiration and model for the protest against the Miss America pageant. Redstockings was another women's liberation group of this era, which is still active today (Figure 1.1). The feminist activists from this group

spread knowledge of vital women's liberation theory, slogans and actions that have become household words such as consciousness-raising, the personal is political, the pro-woman line, sisterhood is powerful, the politics of housework, the Miss America Protest, and 'speakouts' that would break the taboos of silence around subjects like abortion.

> (redstockings.org)

In 1989, their feminist history project, The Archives for Action, made radical women's experiences of the feminist movement widely available.

Feminist activists used methods and theory learned through their experiences as student and civil-rights activists during the anti-Vietnam-war and **New Left** protests. For example, the idea of bra dumping was borrowed from anti-war demonstrations

Redstockings

CATALOG

Women's Liberation Studies Archives For Action

Pamphlets, broadsides, journals, and audiotapes from and about the freedom organizing of the 1960's... and afterwards.

See order form for updated prices

BUILDING ON WHAT'S BEEN WON BY KNOWING WHAT'S BEEN DONE

www.redstockings.org

Figure 1.1 Redstockings

where drafts were dumped into trash cans. White women like Robin Morgan had been active in multiple anti-oppression movements and social-justice movements such as anti-racism, anti-colonialisms, and the anti-war movements of the late 1960s. The feminist protests consisted of consciousness-raising, self-help groups, theory and advocacy groups, and other direct and indirect action groups (Hanisch, 1970). Their goal was to challenge the objectification of women's bodies as sex objects. Many of the second-wave feminist ideas were popularized due to the media coverage given to this protest.

Shulamith Firestone (1945–2012), a member of the New York Radical Women and a central figure in the development of **radical feminism**, was the author of *The Dialectic of Sex: The Case for Feminist Revolution* (1970), which became a very influential Marxist feminist analysis of gender oppression. Firestone argued that women are an underclass whose gender inequality and disadvantage is based on a sexual division of labor imposed by patriarchal societal structures. The concept of patriarchy was popularized by radical feminists who believed that US society is a patriarchy: a social, economic, and cultural system in which fathers have total authority over the family and men have legal authority over women and children; and radical feminists sought to free women from family oppression and male supremacy. The radical feminist critique of the Miss America pageant was based on a structural analysis of the pageant's sexism, racism, homophobia, and the way it exploits women's economic needs.

Radical feminists understood women's oppression as the most fundamental kind of exploitation by male supremacist power relations enshrined in patriarchy. They believed that this was a universal structure of domination and analyzed men as the oppressor class. Marxist feminist analysis also theorized women as an oppressed underclass but did not believe in gendered separatism. They focused their analysis on capitalist negation and economic exploitation of women's reproductive and domestic labor. In contrast to these two feminist theories, which focused on systemic and structural analysis, liberal feminism focused more on obtaining individual rights for women by challenging gender discrimination through legal recourse.

The organization most famous for practice of **liberal feminism** is The National Organization for Women (NOW), which was formed in 1966 and is still the largest liberal feminist organization in the US, focusing on legal and constitutional issues such as civil rights, affirmative action, abortion rights, and ending violence against women through legislation such as the Violence Against Women Act. Concepts of patriarchy, oppression, and sexual revolution were popularized through consciousness-raising groups in the late 1960s and early 70s. The Women's Liberation Movement was associated with the myth of bra burning throughout the world due to global media coverage (Dow, 2003). The symbolic dumping of objects protestors called "instruments of female torture," associated with feminine oppression, such as false eyelashes, heels, mops, pots and pans, high-heeled shoes, curlers, hairspray, makeup, girdles, corsets, and bras into a trash can was sensationalized in the media as "bra-burning" (Hanisch, 1970; redstockings.org; Dow, 2003; Kreydatus, 2008). No bras were actually burnt because the protesters were not able to acquire the necessary fire permit.

Feminist historians have divided feminism into different historical phases, creating a typology of feminism that include three specific phases or feminist waves (Spender, 1983): **first-wave feminism** focused on suffrage from the eighteenth to early twentieth centuries; second-wave feminism from the 1960s to the mid 80s focused on women's bodies as a site of patriarchal control; and **third-wave feminism** challenges second-wave feminism's universal category of "woman," extending a feminism of difference combined with the dissolution of sex–gender distinctions. Third-wave feminism has also been theorized as **postfeminism**, which includes multiple kinds of feminist ideas such as black feminism, postcolonial and **Third World feminisms**, feminist cultural and media critiques, and queer and transgender feminisms.

Second-wave Liberal Feminists vs. Femininity

Second-wave feminism, which emerged in the post-World War II era, generated concepts and strategies to describe and critique women's experiences. The idea of femininity as oppressive and as opposite of feminism emerged out of the Women's Liberation Movement. In 1963, Betty Friedan, a former labor organizer, published *The Feminine Mystique* (1963), which was based upon a survey she had distributed to her university alums. This book became a landmark in the development of second-wave feminism. Freidan challenged the "the cult of domesticity" or the "cult of true womanhood," which propagated the idea of femininity as a natural attribute of women and girls and associated femininity with home and family. According to Katherine Lavender (2009:5), the ideal of the "cult of true womanhood" was prevalent in the lives of nineteenth-century upper- and middle-class white women and defined femininity with the characteristics of piety, purity, domesticity, and submissiveness. This ideology of virtuous femininity was "found in women's magazines, advice books, religious journals, newspapers, fiction—everywhere in popular culture." Mary Dore's (2014) documentary *She's Beautiful when She's Angry* opens up the history of the modern feminist movement between 1966 and 1971. Mary Dore was an activist in the women's movement in the 1970s. She uses archive footage and interviews with feminists active at that time to challenge negative stereotypes of feminists as angry, man-hating women. The documentary begins with the publication of Betty Friedan's book and its impact on mobilizing the women's movement. Friedan built on the French feminist philosopher Simone de Beauvoir's 1949 book *The Second Sex*, which made the radical distinction between gender and sex, arguing that "One is not born but becomes a woman…" (de Beauvoir, 1972:267), i.e. that femininity is culturally constructed and is not a biological fact. De Beauvoir transformed the traditional definition of femininity as an attribute of women's biological sexual difference, which assumes a natural connection between gender and sex and erases the fact that it is possible to be biologically female but to refuse to act in a feminine way. She analyzed how the ideals of femininity produce an ideology of women's "natural" inferiority in order to justify patriarchal domination. After being translated into English in 1953, this book became popular in the early 1960s and was extremely influential for European and US second-wave feminists due to its analysis of sexual difference, inequality, and patriarchy. Her writing began the deconstruction of what has come to be called the sex–gender distinction. In this formulation of the sex–gender distinction, gender refers to the social conditioning of women, the imposition of gendered roles and identities, while sex refers to the biological body. De Beauvoir argues that women are victimized through their bodies, not naturally or inherently, but by the way in which women's reproductive capacity has been given meaning or significance in religious and cultural traditions and in the natural and social sciences such as biology, psychology, and even in Marxism. In other words, through male-dominated systems of knowledge, women's social identity (gender) is reduced to their biological bodies (sex) so that gender appears to equal sex; in this way, social conditioning becomes naturalized by the myth that there are essential biological differences between men and women. In order to challenge mainstream norms or power in society, women have to topple the epistemological basis for patriarchy.

Friedan's *The Feminine Mystique* developed the idea that femininity is a myth promulgated through media representations. The alums she surveyed were her former classmates from Smith College in Northampton, Massachusetts. Smith College is a private, independent women's liberal-arts college founded solely to educate upper-middle-class women. Friedan discovered that many of her former classmates were unhappy with their domestic lives as wives and mothers. This inspired her to explore her personal experiences of discontentment and to interview her classmates and other suburban housewives, as well as researching psychology, media, and advertising. Friedan had been a successful women's magazine editor, which gave her the knowledge she needed to analyze and compare representations of women in US women's magazines from the 1930s to the 50s. In doing so, she found that these magazines play an important role in reproducing femininity in different historical contexts. She called this discontentment or unhappiness "the problem with no name." Friedan's work challenged the then dominant Freudian psychoanalytic account of femininity that located sexual differences in the human mind; and she argued that sexuality, like gender, is not the product of natural essential differences in the psyche of men or women, but culturally constructed and learned. Friedan argued that television advertisements from the 1960s and 70s typically represent women as homemakers and that women's magazines reproduce femininity through the repetition of a number of key themes defining an ideal femininity: how to get and keep a man, how to be and stay beautiful, and all manner of minutia having to do with fashion and food.

Marxist and Socialist Feminism: Capitalism and Patriarchy

Marxist feminists, like Shulamith Firestone, synthesized the ideas of de Beauvoir on women's alienation from her true self, Friedan's work on femininity, and a feminist interpretation of Marxism to argue three points that support a second-wave feminist agenda. First, that femininity is an aspect of patriarchal ideology. Second, drawing on de Beauvoir, they examine how women learn to understand themselves, and what it means to be a woman, through the internalization of patriarchal knowledge; in this way, women are unable to be self-defining and so come to see their own bodies as Other, as alienated. Thus, Firestone argues that just as capitalism alienates workers from the products of their own labor—which go to make profits for the ruling class—so women are alienated from their true selves, and instead they come to define themselves through the myths and stereotypes of femininity, myths which serve the interests

Figure 1.2 Women march for racial and economic equality on Fifth Avenue, New York City, 1970
Source: Archive Photos/Getty Images.

of men and patriarchal power. Given all this, the task of feminism according to Marxist feminists is to challenge the myths of femininity that produce **false consciousness** in women. Feminists in the 1960s and 70s tended to focus on representations of women in the media and how these work to reproduce patriarchal ideology (the rule of men and privileging of masculinity), and how they deploy the myth of femininity in order to make masculine control and domination of women appear normal, natural, and unchangeable. Second-wave feminist activism was effective in establishing institutional change when it came to issues such as domestic violence, unequal pay, affirmative action, rape, and fertility control, but it was criticized for its classism, racism, and heterosexism.

Black and Third World Feminisms: Intersectionality

The first public challenge to second-wave feminism came in 1977 from a collective of black feminists that named themselves **The Combahee River Collective.** As black women, the collective argued that they experience oppression based on race, gender, and class. This is what sociologists now call intersectionality, or intersecting forms of oppression. Further, because many of the women in the collective were lesbians, they also acknowledged oppression based on sexuality. They felt that black women's experiences include simultaneous and interlocking oppressions of race, class, gender, and a heterosexual norm. They argue that what is required for an inclusive feminist agenda is an integrated analysis of power relations that puts intersectional perspectives, such as that of black women, at the center of feminist theory and practice. Many of the group members had been involved in **Third World women's anti-colonial movements** and national liberation struggles, and cultural **nationalist** movements such as the Black Power movement and the Third World Liberation Front; as such, they expressed solidarity with all women of color in the US and in the Third World, and with working people everywhere. In 1981, Cherríe Moraga and Gloria E. Anzaldúa published the anthology *This Bridge Called My Back,* which, along with Hull et al.'s (1981) *All the Women Are White, All the Blacks Are Men, But Some of Us Are Brave: Black Women's Studies,* popularized intersectional and black and Chicana feminisms.

Third-wave Feminisms

By the late 1990s there was a shift to third-wave feminism, which seeks to challenge or avoid the second wave's essentialist definitions of femininity, which often assume a universal female identity that overemphasizes the experiences of upper- and middle-class white women and erases those of others. Third-wave feminism focuses on a more **poststructuralist** interpretation of gender and sexuality, as developed in feminist queer theories, and combines many different types of feminism, including women-of-color feminism, **cultural feminism**, even postfeminism, as well as second-wave feminist perspectives such as liberal feminism, radical feminism, and Marxist or **socialist feminism**. Diane Fuss (1989), Teresa de Lauretis (1991), Eve Sedgwick (1993), and Judith Butler (1990) developed the field of queer theory to problematize gender and sexual-identity categories and destabilize normality and the privileges associated with heterosexual life that are embedded in a wide range of institutions and which project deviance and abnormality on to lesbian, gay, and queer sexualities and lifestyles. Queer activists contest definitive categories to highlight the contingency and shifting boundaries of "normative" sex and gender identities—and they have reclaimed the term "queer" to open a space for sexual and gender minorities opposed to the rigid sexual categories of lesbian and gay studies and identity politics. Queer activists have also highlighted the history of suffering associated with the medicalization of "norms" of sexual identities.

The dissolution of the gender binary prevalent in gender and sex distinctions became prevalent with the popularity of Butler's ideas of gender performativity (Butler, 1990), in which she defines femininity as "a mode of enacting and re-enacting received gender norms" (Butler, quoted in Bartky, 1990:65). Thus, femininity and masculinity come into being by what we do in our everyday lived experience, and beauty rituals are one way of performing femininity in order to fulfill heteronormative gender and sexual roles.

In other words, femininity is a set of learned norms about how to be a woman within a particular culture, and sex and gender are both social constructions, i.e. learned cultural and social norms. Sex differences exist but it is the social meanings that we as a society assign to sex as biological or natural that shape our understanding of gender (Butler, 1990:179). Associating men with masculinity and women with femininity creates gender norms, creating the need for gender policing and surveillance—and transgender beauty pageants can be seen as spaces for performing femininity by dismantling gender structures and norms where femininity is denaturalized and is not attributed directly to women. In this way, masculinity and femininity are used to describe behaviors or attitudes, and this interpretation opens up a broad range of being and doing for all without restricting anyone to narrow definitions of gender and sex norms.

Third-wave feminism provides an analysis of capitalist consolidation of power in media and consumer culture. Media consumer culture has appropriated liberal feminist ideas of choice and empowerment as well as anti-feminist ideologies. Feminist media and cultural-studies theories are part of this third wave that has influenced a shift in feminist theories of beauty in the last decade. A shift has taken place from the language of feminine victimization, suffering, and oppression, to a language of empowerment and resistance. Media and cultural analysis focuses on both beauty and gender as cultural practices that mutually constitute each other. Many feminist media and cultural-studies scholars have focused on women's experiences and practices of beautification as a site for pleasure, enjoyment, leisure, and community. For example, Ann Cahill (2003) describes her experiences of dressing up with her sisters as a shared experience of pleasure and female playfulness, creativity, bonding, and female community. She argues that dressing up is not necessarily done for the male gaze in this specific example (although often this is part of the equation). Cahill characterizes this kind of beauty practice as a space of feminist (inter)subjectivity that includes aesthetic as well as sensual pleasures, as well as women's complicity in such pleasures. Similarly, Monica Moreno Figueroa, while researching Mexican women's negotiation of beauty, writes that "beauty is difficult. It is a resource and a feeling, an unavoidable lure that does different kinds of work: it stabilizes and enables hierarchies" (Moreno Figueroa, 2013:146). Both these feminist accounts speak of beauty practices as creating pleasures and positive feelings as well as negative feelings of self-hatred and shame. The exercise of beauty and femininity that feminists of the second wave find oppressive becomes a source for pleasure and empowerment in third-wave feminist analyses of media and consumer female practices.

Media Consumer Culture: New Sexism, Self-hatred, and Governmentality

In *The Beauty Myth* (1991) Naomi Wolf argues that the expansion of beauty ideologies inscribed in media cultures is a weapon against women's educational and employment advancements in US society, the very gains fought for by second-wave feminists. She characterizes this as a patriarchal backlash against the success of the second-wave women's movement. Susan Bordo uses **Foucauldian** and post-structuralist thought to elucidate how women's subjectivities are formed at the intersections of culture, power, heterosexuality, and gender norms. She explains that "Most beauty product adverts rely on the **heteronormative assumptions** of gendered beauty ideals, where the image of before and after promises finding romance, marital partner and or sexual partner as the way to happiness" (Bordo, 2003:102). Advertisements induce women's desires and their identity, Bordo believes, through consumption—by creating wants and artificial needs through the advertising of goods, experiences, desires, and lifestyles that are tempting to us. Advertisements seek to convey a sense of individual satisfaction brought about by the purchase or use of these products. She examines how women's insecurities are targeted by projecting fantasies of finding a future happiness through self-transformation.

Bordo understands femininity as formed in a dynamic network of power relations that she uses to critique gender formation and regulation. Her understanding of how gendered power relations are maintained moves away from much of second-wave Marxist feminist ideas of femininity as wholly oppressive, and she tells a much more complicated story about the nature of power relations in which subjects are implicated, subjects who themselves maintain gender relations through "self-surveillance and self-correction to norms" (2003: 26–7). Rather than understanding power as a possession of an individual, Bordo analyzes discourses of beauty and body that are produced by media and other institutions, and which shape women's and men's bodies. Advertisements use psychology, scientific knowledge, and rhetoric in order to appeal more effectively to each individual. The consumption of beauty-related products and practices convinces us that we can have the pictured life that we dream about, but at the same time we are aware that the beauty ideals conveyed in media representations by beauty queens, female icons, and celebrities are unattainable. The desire by girls and women to achieve these ideals leads to a dissatisfaction with their bodies and feelings of failure and shame. The internalization of beauty ideals, norms, and standards regulate and shame the self and others, and are implicated in a high incidence of self-hatred, low self-esteem, eating disorders, such as anorexia and bulimia, and negative body image and body dissatisfaction among women of all ages and ethnic groups (Bordo, 2003).

Body dissatisfaction tends to focus on body size, weight, and shape. Slimness is integral to beauty ideals and, for large women, fat stigma is closely associated with perceptions of laziness and a lack of self-control or discipline. Samantha Kwan and Jennifer Fackler (2008), members of Sociologists for Women in Society, who produced a factsheet on "Women and Size," elaborate on multiple forms of discrimination attached to **sizism**. They point out the benefits of collective organizing and challenging the production of knowledge on issues of fat activism: "Fat studies scholars and fat acceptance activists... (put) emphasis on body diversity and the celebration of the fat body encourages a 'body positive' perspective and increased body esteem and satisfaction for women of all sizes" (Kwan and Fackler, 2008). More recently, there has been a trend by beauty corporations to produce an army of beauty writers, experts, instructors, and makeover television programs that "educate" women in the "self-making and managing" techniques that force women to regulate and govern their bodies and mind.

Nicolas Rose, a UK Foucauldian scholar, has extended Foucault's ideas to understand current cultural power relations (1990). He writes about a kind of "self-surveillance" and "self-management" that we all perform as part of what he calls "**governmental neoliberalism.**" This **neoliberalism** is a new mode of statecraft in which market rationales are embodied by self-regulating, self-governing subjects. It positions itself as a moral concept and is often indirectly invoked in moral panics related to family, gender, and sexuality. In current consumer culture, we are validated if we demonstrate capacities of hard work, rationality, achievement, the desire to take control of the future, to take action, and to be independent and enterprising. We are valorized if we can maximize our human capital by planning ahead to fulfill our goals. This idea of the self, called **human-capital theory**, is borrowed from business institutions where these qualities are highly valued.

Gill and Scharff (2011) argue that young women in particular are positioned as ideal neoliberal subjects and thus perform neoliberal femininity (Brown, 2005). Christina Scharf's (2014) research found that her UK and German participants constructed their feminist agency—as self-managing entrepreneurs—in "opposition to the 'othering' of the figure of the oppressed 'Muslim' woman who was a passive victim of patriarchy" and "through distinction from those regarded as lazy, insufficiently hard working and vulnerable." She concludes that Western empowered femininity is founded on the reproduction of class and racial exclusions.

We can see that second-wave and third-wave ideas of femininity have been commodified in order to manage subjects as consumers; beauty companies have appropriated qualities associated with femininity (and feminism) to target women as objects of beauty, as well as subjects who can change and empower themselves by consuming beauty products. This appropriation of feminism by the media has been theorized as an aspect of a postfeminist media landscape by Angela McRobbie, who proposed that it is primarily young middle-class white women who have benefited from reproductive rights and access to education and labor markets due to the successes of second-wave feminism (2009: 15). How do we counter such complicated ways in which beauty norms create our identity?

Naomi Wolf advises women to find new ways of understanding and seeing this corporate systemic manipulation of media representations. She also argues that by making women compete with each other for male attention through the use of the beauty advantage, women fall prey to a patriarchal divide-and-rule strategy. Beauty is a resource and capital more available to some, and it is exchanged for other commodities, so it is fought over in a patriarchal culture. She argues that the standards of beauty create "lookism" and beauty advantages based on a beauty and ugliness dichotomy, where ugliness confers a penalty and beauty confers a premium. Beauty capital refers to this premium that individuals are either defined as having naturally or are able to cultivate.

Economists Daniel Hamermesh and Jeff Biddle (1994), researching the advantages of beauty in labor markets, conclude that a sizable advantage is conferred on workers who are considered good looking. They write that "the size of beauty premium inequality is economically comparable to race and gender gaps in the U.S. labor market" (1994:1174). Applying ideas of second- and third-wave feminism, highlighting the intersectionality of gender, race, nation, and culture, we can analyze and situate contemporary ideas of beauty and femininity exhibited in the Miss America pageant.

Exceptional Miss America, Postfeminism, and Neoliberal Femininity

Due to the second-wave-feminist and Civil Rights protests, the Miss America beauty pageant, a not-for-profit corporation, has changed its public image from a "beauty contest" to a "scholarship pageant." The Miss America website markets itself as an achievement program. We are told that the pageant is the nation's largest provider of women's scholarships, awarding 45 million in cash and scholarship assistance each year, and it encourages thousands of young women to take leadership roles in their communities. It invites women to participate so that they can go to college, prepare for a career, and improve their professional skills. It seemingly promotes career and education over domesticity and family.

The Miss America website defines beauty in terms of grace, refinement, and intelligence, combing education with aesthetic concerns. It seems that the Miss America corporation sees itself as a kind of racially progressive feminist platform to educate and mentor young women. Is this a success of second-wave-feminist activism? In one way, we can see that the feminist slogan "the personal is political" has been appropriated by the organizers, who focus on contestants' ambition, achievement, and careers. Some argue that the pageant has taken the feminist critique seriously. Nowadays, contestants like Nina Davuluri and Theresa Vail articulate a strong purpose and desire careers, individual success, and autonomy. They have integrated popular and second-wave liberal feminist ideas into their identity construction, most importantly those of gender equality and individual choice (Banet-Weiser, 1999). They deploy beauty as a resource and capital that can be exchanged for social mobility and other commodities. One example of such aesthetic capital is the financial rewards of the educational scholarship. It becomes obvious that investing in beauty has paid off for many contestants because it has been a source of individual economic success, as well as an initiation into a media and celebrity network resulting in media capital. On the other hand, it could also be argued that the Miss America beauty pageant has insidiously appropriated feminist themes of empowerment and choice, that it has rendered these as **feminist consumerism**—a corporate strategy that employs feminist themes of empowerment to market products, that shares consumerism's focus on individual consumption as a primary source of identity, affirmation, and social change, and that reformulates feminism as achieved principally through grooming and shopping.

Is the Miss America beauty pageant a space of gender and racial progress, which has allowed some women of color monetary gains in terms of college scholarships—and has it opened doors in the media and fashion industry? Miss Davuluri's narrative highlights individual educational achievement, and it is self-determination that is being rewarded by the judges. So what kind of work is being done by investing in beauty? Naomi Wolf's analysis of beauty as currency is insightful here. Many proponents of the Miss America pageant argue that the financial and cultural opportunities provided by winning the Miss America crown lead to considerable success in a variety of other professions. This raises some interesting questions about how beauty can be exchanged for social and cultural capital. Young women are attracted to the opportunity of social and class mobility, and they desire a scholarship awarded on the basis of physical attractiveness and their proximity to a beauty ideal. In this case, the beauty advantage is the capital accrued due to unearned and earned privilege, and this capital allows access to education by linking academic scholarships to physical attractiveness.

Femininity, Anglo-conformity and Multicultural Diversity

The multicultural gendered norms in beauty pageants can be deployed to articulate national unity, pride and patriotism, and the successful assimilation and incorporation of minorities fought for in the Civil Rights Movement. But the Miss America beauty pageant also highlights popular discontent in the expression of some racist stereotypes on social media sites such as Twitter. As the racial demographics of the US change, promising a people-of-color majority, white conservatives become increasingly paranoid as the fear of loss of control over a common national culture becomes a reality. Race is articulated directly by valuing a white beauty aesthetic, but also indirectly as **anti-black racism** is articulated in exceptionalism: a model-minority myth that is also a demand for conformity to Anglo-American standards.

Miss Kansas 2013, Theresa Vail, one of the contestants chosen by online vote as "America's choice," is visibly white, blond, and blue-eyed, reflecting the traditional European-American beauty ideal. On online social-media sites and blogs, Nina Davuluri as Miss New York was negatively compared to Miss Vail, who many felt was racially more authentic and, as such, should be the one to represent Miss America. The judges may have chosen Miss New York, but the national public chose Miss Kansas. There is no doubt that Miss Vail challenged ideals of femininity by visibly displaying her tattoo; and Miss Vail's job as a sergeant in the military and her archery and hunting hobbies are generally not valued as feminine, but these ideas were appropriated to resonate with narratives of patriotism, and nationalist foundation myths. Miss Kansas was able to persuade the Miss America beauty-pageant online voting public that she embodied US values. Miss Kansas's physical feminine characteristics symbolized the online public's Americanness as a white identity, highlighting the intersectional relations of race, nation, and femininity.

Nations often have a foundational myth, a story that locates the origin of nation, people, and their national character so early that it is lost in a mythic time (Hall, 1992b:274). Hunting and outside sports invoke nature, land, and adventure. Consider Fredrick Turner's frontier thesis (1920:293), that the foundational myth of America is structured by the history of the American West and, more specifically, by its westward expansion. This story portrays hard-working individuals who overcome multiple obstacles, taking grave risks to shape the land and nature in order to transform poverty into profit—a recurrent motif of the American dream (related to the image of Manifest Destiny discussed in the Introduction). In this way, capitalism, economic success, and free-market ideology are integral to the foundational myth of America.

Before the mid 1980s, it was rare to see many women of color participating in the Miss America pageant but that is no longer the case. In an interview with Michel Martin on National Public Radio (NPR), Nina Davuluri elaborates on the similarities between her own crowning and Vanessa Williams's win in 1983:

> Well, first, let me just comment on Vanessa Williams because she was a former Miss Syracuse, and I was also a former Miss Syracuse. We both went on to win the Miss New York title and both two very historic Miss Americas. It was exactly 30 years ago to the date, September 15, we were both crowned. So that's just so surreal, but I was in the same situation… And I'm in the process of applying to medical school right now, and I have zero funds for my education. That was a large part of why I came back to the organization, and I now have a total of $60,000 to put towards that, which is amazing.
> (Interview with Michel Martin on NPR, September 18, 2013).

Here, Nina Davuluri aligns her win with the historical win of Vanessa Williams, pointing to the importance of her win as an aspect of racial progress. She demonstrates racial solidarity with Vanessa Williams as a sign of the importance of the Civil Rights Movement to national pan-ethnic unity. Davuluri's performance of a Bollywood dance (Figure 1.3) was viewed as culturally alien and "foreign" on the social-media platform of Twitter. The dance performance can also be interpreted as demonstrating ethnic pride for South Asian Americans (also referred to as Indian Americans, as opposed to American Indians), especially considering how little cultural visibility South Asian Americans have in mainstream US media.

Figure 1.3 Nina Davuluri's Bollywood fusion dance
Source: Michael Loccisano/Getty Images.

In addition, her interview could be interpreted as a strategic demonstration of **multicultural pluralism**. Here, we can see the different multicultural discourses at play: the first is the liberal multiculturalism of the judges (often chosen from elite groups and institutions), and the winner enacts a discourse of diversity, multiculturalism, and individual achievements. The second multicultural discourse is the conservative multiculturalism of the online audience, focusing on conformity to Anglo ideals and the demand for racial assimilation (Park, 1939; Gordon, 1981). The conservative multiculturalism deploys a traditional assimilation model, where Anglo-conformity is the aim, and where immigrant and minority groups are expected to adapt to Anglo-American culture as quickly as possible. Anglo-conformity has been a precondition for access to better jobs, education, and upward class mobility (Gordon, 1981).

Neither is liberal multiculturalism a benign policy. It reinforces the model-minority stereotype, which has deep roots in a history of race and ethnic relations of divide and rule by comparing and disparaging ethnic groups in their approximation to an assumed superiority of the white majority, granting honorary whiteness to some and excluding others. South Asian Americans are routinely used as a political and cultural weapon in the US media to denigrate working-class black communities. Multiculturalism can be defined as respect and tolerance of cultural diversity or of culturally embedded differences in a society (Parekh, 2000a; Hall, 2001). Liberal multiculturalism privileges the individual focusing on integration and on the idea of mutual tolerance, cultural diversity, and equal opportunity. Conservative multiculturalism, focusing on assimilation, does not validate public displays of cultural difference. It holds that ethnic and cultural difference should be maintained privately—for example, conservatives have campaigned vigorously against linguistic pluralism in public spaces (Hall, 2001).

One of the key problems with ideas of **liberal multiculturalism** (which is prevalent in many national institutions) is the management of difference by prioritizing the celebration of cultural and ethnic differences, as opposed to addressing structural discrimination based on gender, sexuality, race, disability, age, and religion. It is true that this politics of recognition is important in that it has enabled marginalized communities to find a voice. But it is also true that, often, it is minority individuals who are closest to dominant white ideals that are rewarded (see Chapter 2). We can see the **Civil Rights discourses of racial equality and opportunity** appropriated in ideas of liberal and corporate multiculturalism. The anti-racist critique of this diversity agenda is linked to good intentions and comes with wonderful equal-opportunity policies, but it also comes with bureaucratic blocks, tokenism, and institutional statements that promise inclusion and equality, but in reality do not deliver true inclusion.

Many black feminists and race scholars writing on race relations have analyzed Miss Davaluri's accomplishment as a win for racial equality, one that represents a success story of hard work by a second-generation immigrant woman, who, undergoing regimes of training to improve and fashion her body to pass the swimsuit test, overcame obstacles of ethnic difference and racism to win many levels of local and state competitions. Two myths—**the Asian model minority** and American exceptionalism—converge and reinforce the discourse of an American dream and of the US as a nation of opportunity, racial diversity, pluralism, justice, fairness, and democracy. The ideal citizen is an individual who can overcome many obstacles of sexism and racism in order to succeed—a self-improving and self-fashioned individual is the ideal national neoliberal subject. In the "post-racial" Obama era, anti-black racism is expressed in terms of the model-minority myth that is mobilized in **media moral panics** against working-class black Americans, invoking **Cultures of Poverty**, or **cultural pathologies**, focusing on criminality and poverty as individual forms of deviance. The neoliberal discourse of "deserving" and "not deserving" is consolidated so that the poor can be blamed for their poverty, even as an upward redistribution of economic resources (tax cuts for the rich since the Reagan era) is rarely discussed.

The Miss America Corporation constructs its brand as a diversity-loving organization. This is **corporate branding** by crystallizing national characteristics of pluralism and multiculturalism as a US trademark in an easily understood way, and by selecting specific individuals who are seen to embody these values. It is also an excellent example of a colorblind racial ideology that makes individuals of color hyper-visible, as examples of exceptional achievement in a dominant culture that valorizes deserving subjects. The message is that only if you work hard (invoking a Protestant work ethic) can you rise above the structural inequalities of an educational system in crisis. Similarly, a postfeminist analysis also focuses on individually empowered women by highlighting the enterprising nature of particular women's stories. It refuses to recognize power and class position as key constituents in the production of feminine selves such as that of Miss Davuluri. Those, like Miss Davuluri, who are from privileged backgrounds and with the help of family and community are able to overcome sexism and racism and achieve success should be rewarded. But what should also be highlighted are the ways in which individuals draw from the collective labor of social capital for help in achieving that success. The reality of historical and structural discrimination against internally colonized groups such as Native Americans, native Mexican Americans and black Americans, as compared to migrants who entered this country with high levels of economic and educational resources, is erased. Racial inequality and disparity is blamed on cultural and racial pathologies of individual families and (usually and more specifically) mothers. Is the contest open to a vast majority of women of color who are working-class women, who may be unable to afford a team of trainers and the experts needed to fashion a Miss America body? In this way, attention is deviated from a debt-ridden education system and the basic economic unfairness of a workplace where women still earn much less than men for equivalent jobs, and where a national minimum wage is being signed into effect only now. The Miss America beauty pageant is a site for the construction of a neoliberal feminine citizenship where viewers are socialized into US values that are denoted by individuated, enterprising selves that succeed through consumerism. The central focus is on the personal and the individual and not on collective social problems, such as the dismantling and breakdown of the education system.

Nonetheless, Miss Davuluri's win is still a significant affirmation for individual girls and women who form the audience and consumers of popular culture. Her win is also a part of the racially progressive policies fought for by the Civil Rights Movement, second-wave feminism, and black feminists to make the US more democratic and equitable.

Conclusion

In this chapter I investigated the second-wave feminist protests and the rich history of feminisms. The chapter focused on ideas of beauty as capital, to demonstrate why beauty is a commodity that is exchanged for class mobility, thereby influencing women's life chances and opportunities. The chapter examined how Miss America's gendered and racialized body is symbolic of national identity and produces an exceptional neoliberal feminine identity as the ideal national consumer identity for citizens to emulate. I investigated feminist and sociological debates on structural power relations and individual agency in order to problematize notions of choice, freedom, and empowerment. I also examined the ways in which feminism and multiculturalism are appropriated by the neoliberal capitalism of the Miss America Corporation, which propagates brand nationalism, representing the US as a feminist, progressive nation of multiculturalism and gender progress in a bid to consolidate cultural dominance on the global stage.

DISCUSSION QUESTIONS

1. What role does beauty play in the accumulation and exercise of power in society? Why do women, and increasingly men, engage in these practices? How might women resist beauty ideals?
2. Which feminist theories would help you better understand and analyze empowering and disempowering aspects of beauty?
3. How is Miss America's gendered and racialized body symbolic of national identity in the discourses of neoliberalism? What is your understanding of neoliberalism?
4. What different ideas of racial conflicts and tensions are produced when analyzing the Miss America beauty pageant?

II: Black Is Beautiful

Anti-racist Beauty Aesthetics and Cultural Resistance

Introduction

I look different from my cousins. I have dark features, dark skin, dark hair, dark eyes, big nose and lips. And, I used to get made fun of because of how I look. With my cousins, they are light-skinned and my aunts used to say to them, "You are gonna get somewhere!" But (to me) my aunts used to say, "Janet you'll end up nowhere, you are nothing!" I thought I was a mistake and that nobody could see any good in me. I did not talk to anybody because I did not think they would understand me. I tried to hurt myself because I thought I was nothing. I thought I was worthless.

(Janet Goldsboro, 17 years old, in *My Black Is Beautiful*, 2007)

I begin with a quote from the documentary *My Black Is Beautiful: Imagine a Future* (Figure 2.1), directed and produced by Lisa Cortes in 2007. This film focuses on a young black woman struggling with her belief that she is ugly and worthless because of her dark skin and African facial features. The documentary invokes the 1960s Black Is Beautiful social movement and its important message of challenging prevalent colorism in black communities and racism in wider American culture and it was created as an educational and supportive tool for young black girls struggling with self-image and body dissatisfaction. However, Margaret Hunter's (2011) research uncovers that this documentary was sponsored by Procter and Gamble, a billion-dollar multinational company that propagates contradictory discourses on beauty and race. The **commodification** of black musical cultures and the social movement Black Is Beautiful is highlighted in contemporary popular culture. The media campaign attached to the documentary uses language that critiques the domination of white beauty standards, and yet Procter and Gamble sells hair-straightening products to women of color. Hunter (2011:161) points out the contradictions of consumer culture: "They have even co-opted the anti-racist language of Black Liberation movements of the past in order to sell cosmetic products to black women around the globe."

Figure 2.1 Janet Goldsboro (left) and Black Girls Rock! founder Beverly Bond at the *My Black Is Beautiful* premiere, New Jersey Performing Arts Center, October, 2013

Source: Bryan Bedder/BET/Getty Images for BET.

This chapter explores the history of the Civil Rights Movement of the 1960s to contextualize the importance of Black Is Beautiful, and examines if this campaign changed black women's experiences of beauty through the a black feminist framework. If femininity is defined by the absence of blackness, then the role the Black Is Beautiful movement played is one of the most significant anti-racist challenges to the dominant white beauty, destabilizing its cultural power. The global popularity of hip-hop and the musical aesthetic of black pride and **black nationalism** originate in the Black Is Beautiful youth movements.

Black Is Beautiful grew out of the Nation of Islam in the 1950s and became a popular national movement in the 1960s with the Black Power movement. The Civil Rights Movement, which created a cross-generational coalition that included the younger members of the Black Power movement (also known as **the Black Liberation Movement**), sought to challenge not only racism but also colorism, which were consequences of European **colonialism**, slavery, and the prestige hierarchies that were prevalent within the black and non-black communities.

In Chapter 1, I argued that the Miss America beauty pageant sends out messages about who is excluded from beauty and femininity, and that the global beauty standard it communicates is a sexist and racist one. This beauty standard is endorsed and propagated in popular culture by Hollywood film stars, youth-culture icons, and celebrities. Beyoncé Knowles is one such globally popular star who is adored and followed by millions of girls and women as a role model of black femininity and ideal beauty. As a popular celebrity, as a black feminist and feminine icon, and as a successful entrepreneur, Beyoncé has various meanings attached to her star persona, and represents the multiple tensions and paradoxes of global US capitalism. I will analyze her importance in global popular culture as a black entrepreneur and musical artist who shapes global-youth-cultural trends and feminine ideals. The desire of girls and women to achieve these ideals leads to dissatisfaction with their bodies and feelings of failure, shame, rejection, psychic pain, and desire to self-harm. Black role models who validate white beauty ideals are sites of ambivalence, and reinforce contradictory realities of living in a racist and sexist world.

In Cortes' documentary, Janet travels to South Africa to understand her African ancestry and to explore her psychic pain of devaluation, and she comes to an understanding that she can define beauty for her self and negotiate beauty norms imposed by family, media, and popular culture. She comes to an understanding that there are multiple definitions of beauty and that she has a choice to define beauty using different beauty aesthetics, such as **Afrocentric** and Eurocentric.

Dominant beauty standards in the US have positioned and continue to position black girls and women as less beautiful, less feminine, and less human if they possess darker skin and African hair texture and facial features. For generations of black women, the choice of hairstyle such as an Afro was part of political action challenging the devaluation of blackness, black bodies, and black women's beauty. Black women, emboldened by the gains of the Civil Rights Movement, rejected these beauty standards, impacting black youth culture with a politicized feminist consciousness. Maxine Leeds Craig (2002:9), whose extensive research informs this chapter, conveys the importance of beauty rituals in shaping identity: "Racial identities are defined through a continual interplay of individual practices and collective action. Each day of their lives, black women rearticulate the meaning of black racial identity as they position themselves in relations to culturally available images of black womanhood." In the late 1960s, Angela Davis' natural (un-straightened) hairstyle, known as the Afro, was one of the widely circulated images of a black woman. The Afro became a symbol of militant black pride and cultural resistance, promoting an Afrocentric anti-racist beauty aesthetic, but it was also associated with danger, criminality, and rebellion—and Angela Davis was on the FBI's most-wanted list, labeled a dangerous terrorist. In 1970, she was arrested, imprisoned, and eventually acquitted after a massive international Free Angela Davis campaign.

Davis is a lifelong feminist activist, scholar, and continental philosopher, who began her activism in the Black Liberation Movement in the 1960s. She is one of the most respected public intellectuals because she has consistently spoken out against systemic and interrelated forms of multiple oppressions arising out of imperialism, colonialism, and global capitalism. She is well-known for popularizing the notion of a "prison industrial complex" and for her advocacy of an international prison-abolition movement. Ingrid Banks (2000), writing on the importance of hair for black women's everyday lived experiences, opened up a discussion of Angela Davis' Afro, pointing to Davis' own ambivalence about being reduced to a hair-do (Davis, 1974, quoted in Banks, 2000:13). Banks explains that Davis' ambivalence is due to the impact of her image on other black women who wore their hair "natural" in the 1970s when Davis was on the FBI's wanted posters. Many black women with Afros were targets of police repression during the two months Angela Davis was hiding as a "fugitive" (Davis, 1974:42, quoted in Banks, 2000:15).

Drawing on black-studies scholars such as Angela Davis (1974, 1983), Patricia Hill-Collins (1990, 2006), bell hooks (1989, 1992), Robin Kelley (2002), Tricia Rose (1994), Maxine Leeds Craig (2002, 2006), Margaret Hunter (2005), Ingrid Banks (2000), Mark Hill (2002), Cheryl Harris (1995), Aaron Gullickson (2005), Joan Morgan (1999), Denise Noble (2000), Aisha Durham (2007, 2012), Gwendolyn Pough (2004), Whitney Peoples (2008), and many others, I set out to examine the impact of the black pride movement. The slogan "Black Is Beautiful" carved out a space of black pride and cultural affirmation so that a new conception of beauty and consciousness could come into the American imagination. Black feminist consciousness of this beauty protest was shaped by drawing on ideas from the Black Nationalist and Third World women's anti-colonial movements, the New Left, and the anti-Vietnam-War and second-wave-feminist movements of the 1960s and early 70s. Black feminist critique prioritized black women's everyday experiences in the slogan "The Personal is Political." Black pride and nationalism were articulated not only through self-presentation but also through culture, religion, language, and music (Levine, 1978). Soul music like the blues came out of black experiences of suffering and of struggles for emancipation, reconstruction, and full citizenship. Nina Simone's experiences as a soul singer, songwriter, and civil-rights activist have inspired many (Simone and Cleary, 2003; Feldstein, 2005) to recount her struggles challenging US racism. Her daughter Lisa Simone Kelly says that her mother was told many times that "her nose was too big, her lips were too full, and her skin too dark" (Dargis, 2015). Liz Garbus's 2015 biopic *What Happened, Miss Simone?* discusses the importance of Simone's music and activism for the Black Lives Matter movement. Her song *Mississippi Goddam*, sung to Selma marchers in 1965, protested lynching and the murder of blacks by white supremacists, and *Black is the Color of My True Love* celebrated the success of the Black Is Beautiful protest. In the PBS documentary *Many Rivers to Cross*, Henry Louis Gates (2013) proposes that the impact of this protest can be ascertained by the widespread popularity of the television program *Soul Train* (begun in 1971), which broadcast black music such as R&B, soul, funk, jazz, disco, gospel, and later hip-hop to a national audience. Don Cornelius, a black entrepreneur, who owned and presented *Soul Train*, also promoted cultural consumption of the Afrocentric lifestyle, selling black hair products, clothing, fashion, and other products.

Black music was made fashionable and marketed as cool and hip to black and white youth audiences. This combination of politics and cultural commodification of Black Is Beautiful youth culture was very profitable because black consciousness was being marketed as an identity accessory. In the 1990s, Tricia Rose (1994:176) identified the importance of hip-hop, a new art and cultural formation produced by poor and marginalized black youth in the late 1970s, which combined black consciousness with musical and cultural creativity. Rose pointed out that rap and hip-hop culture provided an intergenerational bridge between young black women and men and black feminism. For Patricia Hill-Collins (2006), the pedagogies of black nationalism and black feminism are integral to hip-hop youth and popular cultures and are part of Black Liberation struggles (Kelley, 2002), articulating black experiences resisting racism.

Beyoncé is a key player in global and national popular-cultural meaning—and, considering her significant position in the music, fashion, culture, and beauty industries, can we situate her feminist consciousness at the intersection of these social movements? I will examine the ways in which Black Is Beautiful beauty protests and black cultural nationalism contributed to the contemporary mainstream popular youth culture in which Beyoncé reigns supreme. Beyoncé's importance in popular culture as a black feminine icon can open up an analysis of the importance of social movements in the constructions of national identity. In addition, an analysis of her femininity and feminism can illuminate the imbrication of race, class, gender, and sexuality in the construction of US national identity. Beyoncé's feminist consciousness draws from black cultural consciousness but is also partially shaped by corporate market rationality that appropriates "difference" strategically in multicultural and feminist branding. The incorporation of Black Is Beautiful in a number of consumer marketing campaigns illustrates an intentional misreading of the black feminist critique of capitalism, patriarchy, homophobia, and cultural racism. Drawing on scholarship by Patricia Hill-Collins (2006), Joan Morgan (1999), Gwendolyn Pough (2004), and Aisha Durham (2012), I examine the formation of hip-hop feminism as a new and reinvigorating interpretation of black feminism, challenging the authority of academic feminism as well as that of individual-focused neoliberal feminism, displayed by Beyoncé. Hip-hop feminism combines black feminist critique with the potential of youth hip-hop culture to invite younger women and men into a feminist consciousness.

The History of Black Is Beautiful: Black-nationalism Consciousness and Feminism

The origins of the Black Is Beautiful movement can be traced to the idea of black self-determination and to the ideas of creating a community. **The Great Migration**, the largest internal migration in US history, which occurred in 1910–30 and

1940–70, led blacks to cities like Chicago, Detroit, Milwaukee, Philadelphia, and New York, and created black communities and the conditions for a collective social movement to emerge (Lemann, 1986; Frey, 2004:1–3), drawing on experiences of formerly enslaved leaders from the **abolitionist movement** (Ferrell, 2006). By the 1940s, the Civil Rights Movement was a coalition of many different networks of institutions comprising trade unions, churches, and cultural and social groups. The aim of the movement was to end racial segregation, discrimination, and enforce voting rights. It became nationally known due to a series of protests between 1954 and 1968 (given television coverage), such as the successful Montgomery bus boycott (1955–6) in Alabama (Chong, 2014). Martin Luther King, Jr, was one the best known leaders of the Civil Rights Movement, which used a combination of strategies such as non-violent civil disobedience (as Mahatma Gandhi used in the Indian anti-colonial movement against the British empire) and Christian beliefs of loving the enemy to dismantle racial segregation. The Civil Rights Movement was successful in ending de jure (legal) but not de facto (actual) racial segregation and obtaining voting rights. However, the poverty and structural discriminations that the majority of urban blacks were facing did not change.

The Black Power Movement

The emergence of the Black Power movement (1966–75) occurred in the social contexts of collective discontent of the black underclass, expressed in inner-city riots from 1964 onward (Wilson, 1984; Lemann, 1986; Inniss and Feagin, 1989; Van Deburg, 1992; Joseph, 2006). The Black Power movement charged the Civil Rights leadership for letting down the masses of blacks suffering dire poverty and state racial violence. Black leaders such as Huey Newton of the Black Panther Party, Stokely Carmichael of the Black Power movement, and Malcolm X (initially a member of the Nation of Islam and later founder of the Organization for African Unity) espoused black nationalism, separatism, and the necessity of using violence as a means of black self-defense against racism. Malcolm X (X, 1964) challenged assimilation into white cultural norms and resisted the white paternalism of the liberal left and of the Christian organizations working within the civil-rights institutional structure. In the face of state police and individual racial violence suffered by black people, he criticized Dr Martin Luther King's non-violence strategies.

The Black Power leaders drew their critique of **cultural assimilation** from thinkers like W. E. B. Du Bois (1903, 1935) and Frantz Fanon (1967a, 1967b) and criticized the Civil Rights Movement's attempts to assimilate and integrate black people. Instead, they proposed black nationalism, racial solidarity, and economic autonomy. In the 1960s and 70s, the Black Power movement incited an unparalleled response among young blacks in rejecting racist white ideology and Eurocentric beauty standards by the internalization of Black Is Beautiful, expressing a new racial consciousness. bell hooks (1989) calls this response "the replacing of self-hatred into self-love." The Black Power movement mobilized the idea of our bodies as a cultural resource to generate a new aesthetic and imaginary—to reconstruct black cultural pride. The **Harlem Renaissance** (Lewis, 1995) had inspired the black elites but now it was time to mobilize ordinary working-class black folks. Their attempt to awaken a black cultural identity was thus inextricably tied up in "decolonizing minds and consciousness" so that black culture could be a space of freedom and affirmation for working-class folks without striving to be respectable. Black poets, writers, musicians, singers, and artists produced a new black cultural aesthetic. They explored and rewrote African history and culture, challenging Eurocentric Western knowledge production that characterized Africans as uncivilized, subhuman, and backward. In this way, blackness was given a new meaning and a new symbolism to reconstruct black culture, ethnicity, and identity by mobilizing historical knowledge.

Robin Kelley (2002) elucidates that the idea of black self-determination was crucial to what he calls the black freedom struggles such as the abolitionist movement (Ferrell, 2006), Garvey's Back to Africa movement, **the Pan African Congress**, the Harlem Renaissance, the Negritude, the Civil Rights Movement, the Black Power movement, and the black feminist struggle. The aim of these freedom struggles was to generate a consciousness among African slaves to become aware of themselves as a people, to form a collective identity based on their common experiences. Thinkers in these social movements introduced the ideas of black nationalism and self-governance. Nationalism, as defined by Anthony Smith (2010:5), is an ideology that promotes a nation's well-being. Nations as collectives have goals to create national autonomy, unity, and identity. There are five important aspects to nations: "process of formation and growth; a national consciousness or sentiment; a language and symbolism; a social and political movement; and an ideology" (Smith, 2010:5).

The Decolonization Movement

W. E. B. Du Bois was one of the most influential black leaders, and a sociologist (1868–1963), who thought through ideas of black consciousness, nationalism, and identity in the context of American slavery and Jim Crow segregations. He was also a member of a transnational solidarity movement, the Pan-African Congress, an organization that met in London and Paris to devise racial solidarity against colonialism and imperialism. In his book The *Souls of Black Folk*, written in 1903, Du Bois portrayed the genius and humanity of the black race to argue for full enfranchisement and racial quality. His book was a protest against the inhumanity of lynching, Jim Crow laws, and discrimination in education and employment. He presented his insights into the inner workings of the black psyche as a result of racial violence and segregation, and proposed that African Americans had developed a unique identity shaped by processes of assimilation and separatism that created a double consciousness. He proposed a new way of conceiving humanity from this double-consciousness perspective.

Between 1910 and the 1930s, Marcus Garvey's Jamaica-based Universal Negro Improvement Association (UNIA), with 11 million members of African descent from the Caribbean, the Americas, and Europe, was one of the most powerful Black Nationalist movements, organizing back-to-Africa repatriations (Kelley, 2002). Pan-African leaders such as Garvey, Du Bois, and Anna J. Cooper met annually to discuss strategies to dismantle the European colonization of Africa and to "unify and uplift" people of African descent. The Paris-based urban movement called the Negritude (meaning "black" in French), an anti-colonial movement of African and Caribbean students and intellectuals—Aimé Césaire, Léon-Gontran Damas, and Léopold Sédar Senghor—who, like Garvey and Du Bois, believed that the shared black cultural heritage of members of the African diaspora was the best tool in fighting against European colonialism and domination. They wrote about the value of indigenous cultures, values, and beliefs in their literary, poetic, and philosophical writings, and explored ideas of black humanism. They criticized the hypocrisy of Western philosophies and knowledge production that devalued and denigrated African beliefs, values, institutions, and civilizations (Césaire, 1972). In this sense, they were inspired by the creativity and cultural resistance of the Harlem Renaissance cultural workers. They understood that a new transatlantic black consciousness needed a revitalized culture and history that would free colonized people from white racialized thinking.

The idea of self-governance was also part of the decolonization movements (1945–1970s) of independent nations that opposed European colonialism in many African and Asian countries and came together to form the first global Afro-Asian conference, also known as the Bandung Conference, in 1955, in Indonesia, to promote solidarity through Afro-Asian economic and cultural cooperation. Frantz Fanon, an African-Caribbean psychiatrist and a revolutionary intellectual who joined the Algerian Liberation Front to fight French colonialism in Algeria, was a thinker much influenced by the decolonization movements, who opened up an analysis of "personal" and psychic impacts of racial stereotypes on black and colonized subjects.

"Look a Negro ... Mama, see the Negro! I'm frightened ..." I could no longer laugh, because I already knew there were legends, stories, history, and above all *historicity* ... I was responsible ... for my body, for my race, for my ancestors.
(Fanon, 1967a:82)

This is Frantz Fanon's famous text from his first book, *Black Skin, White Masks* (first published 1952), in which he is faced with the racist gaze of a young white girl who mediates dominant meanings attributed to his black body in French culture. In articulating this account, he examines the ways in which racism, internalized by the colonized, produces an inferiority complex and can result in emulation of whiteness. Fanon argues for the idea of reinventing a black consciousness through a psychological liberation of "self." Personal transformations were seen as a way of liberating oneself from mental slavery to decolonize one's ways of thinking and being. Fanon was a hero for the Black Power movement and the Third World radical students' movements in the San Francisco Bay Area in the 1960s and 70s (San Francisco State University and University of California, Berkeley). Non-violent student activism over a long period of time eventually brought ethnic-studies departments into many universities, subverting dominant knowledge production and rewriting the history, politics, and cultures of minority ethnic communities.

The Black Feminist Movement

Angela Davis (1981), Patricia Hill-Collins (1990), and Robin Kelley (2002) show us that the black feminist movement grew out of the Civil Rights Movement, stemming from groups such as the Student Nonviolent Coordinating Committee, and the Black Power movement, including the Black Panther Party (founded in 1966) and several radical black feminist women's organizations founded between 1966 and 1970 (Kelley, 2002). Black women were organizing and leading the strikes, labor unions, boycotts such as the bus boycott initiated by Rosa Parks, sit-ins, marches such as the March on Washington, and other important civil-rights campaigns, as well as many community-based programs such as free health programs and free breakfast programs for the Black Power movement. However, their experiences were often subsumed in the category of black people in the Black Nationalist movement and in the universal category of women in the women's movement.

Black women's experiences of poverty, misogyny, sexism, and racism were glossed over and often not even acknowledged in these movements. The black feminist movement not only grew out of these movements, it actually formed due to opposition and resistance to sexism and racism within them. Black feminists felt marginalized by the Black Nationalists, who tended to embrace patriarchal values and often relegated women to traditional roles of mothering and caretaking, while the racism of white feminist organizations meant that black women's experiences of racism, work, family, patriarchy, and state violence differed from white feminists and were therefore ignored as not constituting women's struggles. Black feminist theorists such as Angela Davis, bell hooks, and Patricia Hill-Collins promote a structural analysis of macro and micro power relations of capitalism, patriarchy, and consumer culture, simultaneously producing racism, sexism, heterosexism, and classism in black women's everyday lives. They and many other black feminists have developed black feminist thought as a radical and revolutionary ideology from the first feminist statement produced in 1977 by the Combahee River Collective.

Contemporary Black Culture

In this section, I situate the ways in which feminist and cultural nationalist ideas have manifested in contemporary black US culture. Hip-hop culture is understood by black activists, feminists, and intellectuals as a site of black racial solidarity and consciousness, but it is also a contradictory space of commodification of black women's bodies, and there is much controversy in black academic feminism on this topic. According to Derrick Aldridge (2005:208), hip-hop is "a social youth movement providing a new form of black social critique and (also extends) the ideology of civil rights generations in advocating racial solidarity, community empowerment, and liberatory education." Hip-hop and rap began as a youth musical subculture in the South Bronx neighborhood of New York in the late 1970s, in racially segregated, economically marginalized, impoverished African American and Latino communities (Rose, 1994). Hip-hop and rap told painful stories of urban poverty and alienation from a youth point of view, yearning for a better future. Aldridge explains that rap and hip-hop draw from many black musical traditions such as spirituals, the blues, and the call-and-response style. Hip-hop became a global youth culture by the 1980s due to its being commodified as an urban "black style" in the mass media. Now, hip-hop encompasses rap music, videos, fashion, dance, language, and films. The conflation of real-world problems with authenticity, and blackness, is sold as part and parcel of hip-hop marketing strategy. In arguing for the community empowerment of rap and hip-hop, Aldridge (2005:230) calls out politically conscious rappers such as Sister Souljah, KRS-One, Meshell Ndegeocello, Public Enemy, Michael Franti, and dead prez.

Tricia Rose (1994) chronicles the contribution of women to the evolution of hip-hop culture, especially rap music. Layli Phillips, Kerri Reddick-Morgan, and Dionne Patricia Stephens (2005) also stress the importance of hip-hop as the site of young black women's oppositional consciousness and the significant contribution of black women rap artists in the development of hip-hop and rap. According to Patricia Hill-Collins (2006), hip-hop is a new racial formation which has the potential as a contradictory site of working-class youth-cultural resistance, global capitalism, sexism and black feminist consciousness to challenge racism.

The Impact of Black Is Beautiful on Black Feminine Identity

Afro Pride

Hair is an essential aspect of black women's beauty, and for some the Afro was simply a fashion statement; but for many others, to wear an Afro, braids, or dreadlocks communicated a political message about their identity. Afro signified racial pride and solidarity with Black Liberation movements. Maxine Leeds Craig (2002, 2006) and

Ingrid Banks' (2000) ethnographic research examines the importance of hairstyles to black women's experience of beauty and identity. Craig (2002:5) points to the fact that black beauty contests were held in many communities and campuses during the height of the Black Power movement (Figure 2.2). The black pride movement created cultural awareness of issues of gendered colorism in black communities by challenging internalized racism. Both scholars highlight the complex politics of beauty and challenge the meanings attached to hair in debates on "assimilation and self-hatred hypothesis" connected to straightening or relaxing hair as always being about "mimicking whiteness."

They show that there are multiple varying cultural meanings that black women and girls assign to their hair and their everyday beauty practices in the process of their identity formations. Banks (2000:17) examines hair as a way of understanding "beauty, power, and black women's consciousness and … the multiple realities that black women face … (and) what it means to be black and female in a racist and sexist society." Through an analysis of the interviews, Banks demonstrates the symbolisms and meanings attached to black hair practice. She explains (2000:148) that black women she interviewed "use hair as a medium to understand complex identity politics that intersect along the lines of race, gender, class, sexuality, power, and beauty." Both scholars investigate racial consciousness, political solidarity, and generational and class differences.

According to Maxine Leeds Craig (2002:128), natural tightly curly hair was considered shameful within US black communities, and gendered socialization for girls included learning grooming rituals of straightening their hair from an early age.

Figure 2.2 Miss Black Denver beauty contest, July, 1969. Front row, from left: Julia Sistrunk, 18; Kathy Abernathy, 19; Doris Thomas, 21; Judy Benton, 17; center row: Sondra Francis, 20; Florence Ayers, 22; Sherri Baucom, 22; Mary Gilmore, 18; Doris Boyd, 17; back row: Melodene Alexander, 17; Beverly Flentroy, 22; Joyce Canaday, 19, and Billye Coleman, 20

Source: The Denver Post via Getty Images.

For many black women, hair straightening was not an attempt to look white but "? essential part of black women's communal and social lives, as well as an important step in an black girl's coming of age" (2002:30). Craig, a US sociologist, provides an analysis of black beauty parlors and interviews with individual women, and comes to an understanding of a direct link between hair-straightening grooming practices and the desire for class mobility and middle-class respectability. Craig explains that the performance of "respectability" by "looking like a lady" was a strategy that black women have deployed to counter racist stereotypes of black women to access privileges reserved for white women only. Craig (2002:129) elucidates that the "racial uplift" (stemming from the rhetoric of Negro uplift from the **Reconstruction Era**: Gaines, 1996) pressured women into ideals of respectability. This ideology, also visible in contemporary culture in the Obama era, was initiated by black intellectuals and elites who desired to "uplift the race" by correcting the "bad" traits of the black poor and black women as bearers of black culture. Craig (2002:130) points out that black leaders, politicians, and writers emphasized that women were the upholders of the black race and culture against the smears and slanders of white racists and each woman's appearance and behavior reflected the good character of the race. In addition, for many working women, getting their hair straightened in beauty parlors also provided a much needed space of leisure and female bonding. She suggests that black women consumers helped shape the meaning of black beauty culture in that a trip to the beauty shop gave working-class black women, who spent their days caring for others, the chance to be "pampered and given respect."

Cheryl Thompson's (2009) empirical interviews with eight black women explore the relationship of hair with physical attractiveness and sexuality. She also highlights the difficult and conflictual choices women make between "relaxing hair," "weaving or braiding their hair," and "going natural." The penalties of their choices—"limited employment opportunities; lack of male interest (courtship); and the possibility of their sexuality being questioned" (2009: 854)—impacted their well-being. For Shirley Tate (2007:301), beauty hierarchies and anti-racist aesthetics in the UK for black women illuminate the tensions and conflicts in black women's hair choices, resting on three oppositional binaries:

> the natural/unnatural black, good/bad hair, and the authentic/inauthentic black. The dominant white aesthetic resting on a black/white binary is compared to the anti-racist aesthetic that valorizes "dark skin" and "natural afro-hair" as authentic and natural as the ideal of "natural Black beauty."
>
> (Tate, 2007:302–3)

She highlights the dilemmas and anguish that bi-racial or mixed-heritage women face because of not falling neatly into these binaries and the consequences of having to manage belonging in both groups.

Positive Body Self-esteem and the Problem with the Self-hatred Hypothesis

Sociology and social-psychology research is divided on the importance of the Black Is Beautiful movement. In the 1960s, in social psychology, a belief that a racist environment of segregation and inequality was psychologically damaging, causing low self-esteem in black children, was prevalent. Daniel Moynihan's (1965) report *The Negro Family: The Case for National Action* blamed the continuity of black matriarchy as a reason for the "pathology" of black families originating on the slave plantation. This Cultures of Poverty argument victimized blacks by focusing on broken black family structure and personality dysfunction and played into the hands of conservatives and racists.

In the late 1970s, Robert Simmons (1978) challenged black self-hatred theory by highlighting twelve different studies that used different self-esteem measures. Simmons rightly challenged the bias of researchers who expected to find black self-hatred, which he believed deeply influenced the ways in which research was framed theoretically. Black self-hatred theory had the problem of seeing African Americans as being without agency. Simmons argued for the success of Black Is Beautiful in some contexts: if black children were surrounded by self-affirming caretakers, parents, teachers, and significant others then black children did not necessarily demonstrate low self-esteem. Considering that our idea of self is influenced by positive and negative validation by people who are significant in our lives and who are close to us, this was a reasonable challenge to a generalized self-hatred thesis. In addition, he suggested that a critique of systematic structural racism and discrimination, encouraged by the militant black pride ideas, also helped in externalizing anger and therefore protecting self-esteem.

This internalization of Black Is Beautiful by black women between 1960 and 1990 is highlighted in social-science research investigating black women's greater body satisfaction. For example, Bond and Cash's (1992:885) research into African American college women's perception of self and body image reveals that a majority "felt satisfied with their skin color, irrespective of how light or dark they actually were, and they demonstrated higher levels of body image and self-esteem" when compared to whites, which seem to be linked to more flexible conceptions of beauty and rejections of white ideals. Black women's ambivalent relationship to conforming to dominant beauty ideals and deployment of an African-centered model of beauty, as well as a Eurocentric aesthetic, was a finding in Sekayi's (2003) research, which investigated the impact of the Eurocentric beauty standard on black college women. Cynthia Frisby's (2004) empirical research investigating the impact of mass media on black women's self-esteem and body shape found that black women dismissed images of attractive white women as unimportant but were negatively affected by images of attractive black women. Imani Perry's (2006) research reveals that there has been a decline in the market for skin-bleaching products in the US, which were prevalent until the 1960s. She believes that this could be due to the influence of the black pride movement.

Light-skin Privileges

Contrary to this view, Evelyn Nakano Glenn (2009) argues that the new racial awareness of the 1960s brought little change in skin-color discrimination in the black community. Glenn argues that most black (and white) Americans find dark skin undesirable and value a light complexion. Glenn and Hunter (2005) both offer research proving that women with darker skin are discriminated against in black communities and lose out to their lighter-skinned sisters in both economic and marriage opportunities. According to them, the Civil Rights and Black Power movements did not permanently alter long-standing Eurocentric color preferences among black Americans. Although the Black Is Beautiful movement challenged white standards of beauty, skin-color discrimination did not disappear in the black community.

Scholars researching the impact of Black Is Beautiful on racism, colorism, and skin-color evaluation and discrimination point to an uneven and contradictory picture. It is clear that blacks of mixed heritage accrued patterns of advantages and class mobility by emulating whiteness. Aaron Gullickson (2005), investigating skin-color hierarchy, elaborates on the history of benefits of being "near-white" that mixed-raced blacks accrued through miscegenation and the one-drop rule. The one-drop rule defined people as black if they had "one drop" of black ancestry by highlighting their difference from those with African ancestry. Structural advantages included access to more skilled work (working as a manager of others), access to education, and sometimes freedom from slavery, allowing class mobility for a small group. These advantages were used to deny opportunities to darker blacks by the black elites, who put into practice the "brown paper bag test," where blacks darker than a brown paper bag were denied membership of elite-controlled organizations in the early twentieth century (Russell *et al.*, 1992).

As Russell *et al.* (1992:58) have pointed out, light skin is considered not only more beautiful, but also more feminine. Black women, in order to fit in, and to appear respectable, as well as desiring to be feminine and attractive, felt compelled to imitate whiteness—often painfully, through beauty aids such as skin bleaches, hair dyes, and straightening combs (Russell *et al.*, 1992). Toni Morrison's (1970) character of the young girl Pecola in her novel *The Bluest Eye* is a poignant illustration of the painful inner journey that many young black girls (and girls of color) undertake, even today. Pecola's desire for white skin and blond hair was backed up by her real-life understanding that if she were white she could escape poverty and suffering.

Mass-media and popular-culture images of female sexual attractiveness also rein-force skin-color discrimination by valorizing black women with lighter skin as sexu-ally desirable and sexually attractive. Black celebrities, such as Beyoncé, who imitate "white" standards of feminine beauty, reinforce racist beauty norms. Despite the gains of the Civil Rights Movement, therefore, Margaret Hunter (2005:49) argues that "European colonization and slavery have left a lasting imprint on African American and Mexican American women through the skin color hierarchies that privilege light skin over dark skin." Her research (2005:57) on lighter-skin privileges among black and Mexican American women demonstrates that skin-color stratification is very much a current social problem. She explains that the privileges of lighter skin are "learning, earning, and marrying more." The association of cultural ideals of whiteness with structural access to opportunities has been the key to understanding why blacks may have internalized racist beauty standards. The association of shame and psychic trauma with darker skin color and African hair and facial features was imposed by a dominant racial ideology enforcing beauty and femininity as white within the African American community. Cheryl Harris (1995), a legal race scholar investigating how rights in property law are intertwined with race, recounts the painful story of her grandmother who was defined as a black woman with white features under the "one-drop rule" and who, when faced with poverty in the 1930s, made a decision to "pass as white" to gain employment at a major retail store. Harris illustrates the privileges embedded in whiteness and theorizes whiteness as a "treasured property" or an asset in a society structured by a racial caste system. Craig (2006) points out that this color-coded criterion demonstrates how class and race come to form a caste along color lines within black life. According to Mark Hill (2002:80), the result of the mainstream racist ideology has meant that black men adopt Eurocentric beauty standards and conflate femininity and sexual desirability with lighter skin, and darkness with mascu-linity and male sexual virility. He proposes that the gendered colorism impacts black women's lived reality psychologically and economically.

Beyoncé's Version of Black Feminist Consciousness

On August 25, 2014, at the MTV Video Music Awards, Beyoncé proclaimed to millions of her fans nationally and globally that she is a feminist (Figure 2.3). She included video of Nigerian feminist author Chimamanda Ngozi Adichie's TED Talk *We Should All Be Feminists!* as part of her song and dance performance. Beyoncé's declaration of being a feminist can be seen as "talking back" to black feminist bell hooks' labeling of her as an "anti-feminist." hooks criticized Beyoncé as a "cultural terrorist," who uses sexualized images of herself to culturally assault young girls who celebrate her as a sign of black feminine success. Beyoncé's performance of a black female character as a slave in a dominatrix narrative in her video "Partition" generated

Figure 2.3 Beyoncé's *Feminist* performance at the 2014 MTV Video Music Awards at The Forum, Inglewood, California, August, 2014

Source: Jason LaVeris/FilmMagic.

this criticism. In an online panel discussion at the New School, *Are You Still a Slave: Liberating the Black Female Body?*, bell hooks, Janet Mock, and Marci Blackman (2014) debated the social problem of sexualization of black women's bodies in mass-media images. According to Marcy Blackman, "Beyoncé is colluding with the patriarchal music and media industry and making money out of a 'porn-style sexiness' because sex sells in music videos." hooks' contention is that Beyoncé's image assaults young black girls' ideas of beauty and sexuality with racist and sexist stereotyping. However, according to Janet Mock, a transgender feminist activist, "Beyoncé showing her ass, owning her body, and claiming that space" is an inspiring performance for a black woman, because she is in control of her sexuality and gives pleasure to her fans. For hooks, Beyoncé is complicit with the "white supremacist, capitalist, patriarchal" visual-media (television and videos) industry's stereotyping of black women's bodies. Her use of these culturally known stereotypes amounts to terrorizing young girls' sexual socialization, who adore her as a role model.

Beyoncé deploys a number of discourses in cultivating her image, music, and star persona. In this aspect, Beyoncé can be understood as combinations of scripts rather than as one person. These scripts use ideas of feminist empowerment, race consciousness, beauty, and sexual empowerment, as well as that of a black woman being in control of her vast business empire. As a black entrepreneur, she is one of the most successful black women, one of the highest earning feminine icons in mainstream US culture. Beyoncé's black femininity opens up a number of discourses on skin-color hierarchy and light-skin privileges we have already discussed.

Beyoncé is not only a product of hip-hop music's global reach, she is also a cultural producer contributing to the music, beauty, and fashion industries. In addition, she owns and manages her own music- and video-production companies, as well as owning other fashion and perfume franchises. The multimillion-dollar global hip-hop music industry has expanded beyond music into videos, fashion, film, and other lifestyle cultural-consumption industries, which has increased black women artists' participation and power. The hip-hop genre is also an important site for young black women's socialization in popular culture of which Beyoncé is the queen. She began her career in an R&B girl group, Destiny's Child, and became famous for her choreography of sexy dance moves focusing on her buttocks, and catchy songs characterized by themes of relationship conflicts and sexual pleasure, as well as feminist empowerment in songs such as *Single Ladies* and *Girls Run the World*. Now she is a solo artist who combines different musical genres such as pop, funk, rap, and soul music in her performances. She also uses multiple media platforms to present her dancing, singing, beauty, and sexuality as performance. She has won numerous Grammy awards and sold millions of records to become the highest-paid black artist of all time (MTV). The *Guardian* newspaper named her Artist of the Decade.

Beyoncé's feminist consciousness comes from rap and hip-hop youth-cultural formations. Phillips *et al.* (2005:255) examine women's rap music from 1976 to the present, and present a long history of black feminist thinking within rap, and hip-hop lyrics by women artists who demonstrate a feminist consciousness in articulating themes of fighting sexism and patriarchy in empowerment lyrics of self-help and sisterly solidarity, as well as of racial solidarity with black men. Women's feminist consciousness is developed through lyrical messages. They give the example of Queen Latifah's (1993) feminist anthem, *U.N.I.T.Y.*, a good example of female empowerment, challenging sexist language and addressed women directly to counter sexism and disempowering media messages.

Beauty as "Racial Capital"

Beyoncé was named as the world's most beautiful woman by *People* magazine and was named by *Time* magazine as one of the hundred most influential people in the world in 2013 and 2014. As we explored in the beginning of this chapter, Beyoncé embodies a contradictory position affirming oppressive white beauty standards as a black woman and as a feminist. Her lighter skin and blond hair reinforce whiteness as a site of femininity and beauty. According to Margaret Hunter (2011:145), "racial capital" is an embodied resource due to our skin color, facial features, hair, and body shape, and is attached to white/Anglo bodies as embodying higher status due to existing racial hierarchies. She explains that it is because we live in a racist society that racial capital is a source of advantage in how we are perceived, and does not depend on how we define ourselves. The concept of racial capital is connected to the larger systems of racism and colorism in the context of commodity culture and the importance of beauty for women's identity. One of hooks' critiques is that Beyoncé endorses unattainable white beauty ideals conveyed in media representations; and, drawing on Margaret Hunter's work, we can analyze that Beyoncé's beauty ideals may be reinforcing racism and colorism. Gendered colorism reinforces sexual desirability as an aspect of femininity attached to skin colors of white or lighter female bodies.

Hypersexuality vs. Sexual Empowerment

Black feminists such as Hill-Collins (2009) and hooks (2000) have noted a historical pattern of representing black female sexuality as inherently "excessive" and "deviant." hooks (2005:96) argues that from Sarah Baartman through Josephine Baker's famous banana dance to Tina Turner's "savage sexuality," black women's bodies are objects of exotic and racial fascination focusing on extreme and disproportionate sexuality. bell hooks (2000:95) also observes in her analysis of black women singers that many cultivated their media image of being sexually available, and this is certainly true of many women in the highly sexualized music industry. In order to gain and maintain any media attention, black women singers like Beyoncé have to self-sexualize to compete with other performers.

Contemporary hip-hop videos, specifically "booty" videos, focus on women's dancing prowess using their buttocks, which represents hypersexual black femininity. Denise Noble (2000) argues for the agency of black female performers in dancehall music videos in the context of UK black club practices. She suggests that representations of black women's sexuality in music videos in mass-mediated popular culture open up an important public space, celebrating the black female body and black femininity, which are given center stage in defiance of dominant images of white femininity as the standard of beauty and privilege in mainstream popular culture. However, these representations, she points out, also produce paradoxical anxieties for those who want black women to be viewed as respectable within the wider society. Noble is pointing to the constraints of the politics of respectability that operate as a politics of silence around issues of sexual pleasure for black women, for the fear of triggering ubiquitous mainstream cultural stereotypes of excessive and deviant sexuality.

Aisha Durham (2012), a feminist media-studies scholar, observes that Beyoncé's iconicity as the queen of the music industry can be explained by her performance of multiple black feminine identities in music videos. She analyzes Beyoncé's video *Check On It* as a sexually liberating space for her audience due to her performance of multiple representations of black sexualities and femininities in a single performance. She explains that Beyoncé sets up a good–bad girl or lady–ho dualism, where she is sexually objectified and simultaneously in control of her sexual pleasure, portraying black femininity as a site of agency. Her crossover appeal to young women, men, and both heterosexual and queer audiences is because she affirms erotic and sexual pleasure by representing diverse sexualities. Durham (2012) explains that Beyoncé may also see herself as bridging class differences by expressing "the culture of silence and middle-class respectability" that constrains lived experiences of black girls and women as well as positive representations of a "nasty girl" who takes pleasure in her sexuality.

Beyoncé's Version of Feminism

Beyoncé's racial and gendered empowerment draws from black musical consciousness such as soul, rap, and hip-hop culture's lyrical black consciousness. She draws inspiration from black singers and performers such as Josephine Baker, Tina Turner, Michael Jackson, and Diana Ross, from successful television hosts such Oprah Winfrey, and from politicians such as President Obama. In this aspect, she represents a space of gender and racial progress and a successful racial assimilation and incorporation into the American dream. This image of an ideal and exceptional black femininity is used as a symbol of the American dream, a sign of democratic multiculturalism, where individual achievement is most valued. In this formulation, a successful model American identity is that of a middle-class black minority.

Beyoncé's feminism is drawn from a number of sources such as black popular culture, rap and soul's feminist empowerment style, liberal feminism, and a black entrepreneurial discourse. As a global feminine icon, she arouses multiple affiliations and sexual desires in her audience. She converts her beauty and sexual attractiveness, as embodied and material assets, into feminine capital. She has also converted her black femininity and now feminism into one of the most successful national brands. According to Catherine Rottenberg (2014:1), there is a new kind of feminism being revived in the US media and therefore in the public domain, where successful women discuss gender equality and inequality. Beyoncé is one of these successful women reviving the much needed discussion of feminism in popular culture for the young women who make up the majority of her audience. However, Rottenberg explains that the recent discussions of feminism by Chief Operating Officer at Facebook, Sheryl Sandberg, in her book *Lean In* (2013), and the first female director of policy planning at the US state department, Anne-Marie Slaughter, in her article *Why Women Still Can't Have It All* (2012), communicate an understanding of gender inequality which rests only on individual successes and failures of highly successful middle-class women and erases the collective experiences of the vast majority of working-class black women and or women of color suffering economic and structural inequalities. She claims that these women propagate a misunderstanding of feminism as an individual project and also a neoliberal view of subjectivity (see Chapter 1). Beyoncé's modern-day feminism is a part of this trend of neoliberal feminism. Neoliberal feminism borrows from liberal feminist ideas of gender equality and individual choice. The media stories of Beyoncé's identity often rest on her individual empowerment, highlighting the enterprising nature of her hard work and risk-taking. These stories also portray Beyoncé as a "sexual entrepreneur" (Harvey and Gill, 2011:52) who uses her sexual capital to gain success in the capitalist and patriarchal music industry. She uses a number of themes attached to sexual empowerment to promote a new, liberated, fulfilled feminist identity for women. In addition, she actively promotes consumer culture, which employs feminist themes of empowerment to market beauty and fashion products, and she reformulates feminism as achieved principally through shopping in consumption of beauty, fashion, and sexuality.

Conclusion: Hip-hop Feminism

This chapter opened up an analysis of beauty as social oppression and inequality, as well as a site of anti-racist resistance to racism, colorism, and sexism. I set out to examine the history and the impact of the Black Is Beautiful campaign as an aspect of wider black freedom struggles. Black freedom struggles of the 1960s reconstructed black culture and consciousness, ushering in a new black identity. Black Is Beautiful changed the values assigned to blackness by mobilizing racial and cultural pride through an increased interest in African ancestry, black nationalism and black feminist consciousness. Black pride and Afrocentric frames of knowledge shifted black men and women's self-evaluations, but this campaign did not erase racism and the resulting internalized racism and gendered colorism. We see the impact of this movement in black women's flexible conceptions of beauty formed by negotiating Afrocentric and Eurocentric beauty ideals. I examined the different meanings attached to hairstyles in black women's experiences of beauty and identity and in debates on "assimilation and self-hatred hypothesis" connected to straightening or relaxing hair. The incorporation of Black Is Beautiful and black musical cultures in a number of consumer marketing campaigns illustrates the profitability and thus the appropriation of black culture as a site of authenticity. The chapter saw how Beyoncé's feminism is partially shaped by corporate market rationality that appropriates "difference" strategically in multicultural and feminist branding. I concluded the chapter with the potential of hip-hop feminism to combine black feminist critique with hip-hop culture to invite and mobilize younger women and men into a feminist consciousness and democratize feminisms. There is no doubt that gendered colorism and the politics of black hair still impacts the life chances of black women. Hip-hop culture is a site of black racial solidarity and consciousness, but it is also a contradictory space of commodification of black women's bodies. But there is hope in the contradictory nature of popular culture, which has the potential to offer solutions to everyday problems. Whitney Peoples (2008) explores the emergence of hip-hop feminism, which is forming a bridge between second-wave black feminist thought and hip-hop culture by elaborating on the writings of two hip-hop feminists, Joan Morgan (1999) and Gwendolyn Pough (2004). Both want to extend a new black feminism and explain that the second-wave black feminist agenda has been ineffective in reaching vulnerable young black women by persistently focusing on misogyny and not enough on hip-hop as a site of black consciousness. Both want to shift the production of feminist thought from the academy to the **public sphere**—an interactive space of media, street, and the home. They coined the term hip-hop feminism to express an urgent need for a new kind of black feminism for the younger generation, both for men and women, as a "public pedagogy" where hip-hop feminism can simultaneously provide a feminist critique of hip-hop as well as use its oppositional consciousness to engage in "dialogue" in black life and culture. They suggest that the lyrical feminist consciousness of black musical traditions, specifically rap and hip-hop, can be mobilized to effect personal transformation, political education, and racial solidarity to rebuild coalitions across differences of class, gender, and sexuality in the black community.

DISCUSSION QUESTIONS

1. In what ways did the Black Nationalist movement challenge and overturn white cultural racism? How has the shifting of structural power relations between the majority white culture and the minority black community impacted black women's self-evaluations?

2. How has "middle-class respectability" socialized black women into desiring racialized beauty standards and femininity?

3. How do you understand the "complex" politics of beauty related to skin color and hair choices? What problems can you see with the self-hatred hypothesis? How can we challenge racism and colorism attached to the idea of racial capital in popular culture?

4. Do you think that Beyoncé is reinforcing racist and sexist stereotypes of black women as hypersexual in "booty" videos, or is she empowering women by her sexual expressions? Is Beyoncé a feminist or an anti-feminist, as bell hooks proposes?

5. What is hip-hop feminism? Can we can create a new black feminist movement?

III: Globalization, Indian Beauty Nationalism, and Colorism

Class, Caste, and Gender Stratification

~~~~✕~~~~

Introduction

In 2003, an advertisement referred to as "the airhostess ad" for a facial-lightening cream, Fair and Lovely, was taken off the air due to protests by a feminist organization, the All India Democratic Women's Association, who defined it as sexist and racist. On July 24, 2003 BBC South Asian news reported, "India debates 'racist' skin cream ads." This cream is the most popular whitening cream sold by the multinational Hindustan Lever Limited. This news article described the advertisement as

> show[ing] a young, dark-skinned girl's father lamenting he had no son to provide for him, as his daughter's salary was not high enough—the suggestion being that she could neither get a better job or get married because of her dark skin. The girl then uses the cream, becomes fairer, and gets a better-paid job as an air hostess—and makes her father happy.
>
> (BBC News, July 24, 2003)

Although this advertisement was banned, there are many advertisements selling products to lighten skin for Indian women, such as Olay's Natural White skin cream and Pond's White Beauty, which promise a natural white skin color (Figure 3.1). These whitening creams are endorsed by Bollywood female film stars and celebrities who are followed as role models of beauty and successful femininities by millions of adoring fans. Nina Davuluri (the Miss America winner) also highlighted this issue and explained that darker skin color like hers was a beauty stigma in India, the country of her parents' origin, where the majority of people are of different tones of darker skin color. She would not have won a beauty contest in India because of her dark skin. The rise of consumer capitalism in India means that women (more than men) are being targeted by the million-dollar skin-lightening and bleaching industry (Parameswaran and Cardoza, 2007:216).

Euro-American beauty corporations seek new and larger middle-class markets around the world to increase their profits through transnational media and cultural

Figure 3.1 Whitening creams sold in India

Source: Prashanth Vishwanathan/Bloomberg via Getty Images.

flows instituting Western **commodity capitalism** in many developing economies like that of India. In Chapter 1, I demonstrated the ways in which consumption practices associated with global beauty pageants play a key role in the reproduction of gender and national identities. Usha Zacharias (2003:398), a feminist cultural-studies scholar investigating emergence of consumer television, claims that there is a new kind of cultural citizenship that symbolizes India's economic transformation since liberalization in 1991. She argues that "whiteness, whitened bodies, and hybrid foreign bodies," signify consumer empowerment and global capitalist progress. The key aim of this chapter is to examine the role of beauty pageants and the beauty industry in normalizing lighter skin as a sign of beauty status. Consumption of skin-lightening creams and middle-class aspirations is linked to discourses of **modernization**, Westernization, and progress.

In 2009, the Dark Is Beautiful campaign was initiated by Women of Worth (WOW), a feminist non-governmental organization, which raises awareness about the widespread prejudice and discrimination facing darker-skinned Indians, specifically in marriage selection and in employment (Rajesh, 2013). It challenges the **normalization** of lighter skin as beautiful and as a site of upward economic mobility, specifically its association with values of success, competence, goodness, and purity. Dark-skin stigma induces internalized shame and psychological damage for female self-worth, and has long been a source of stigma for Indian women, originating in Hindu religious and cultural customs. Many of the dominant revered Hindu deities, such as Ram and Krishna, are represented as having dark skin (painted blue) in popular calendar art. Kali is a female mother goddess who is dark; however, she does not represent ideal femininity for Indian women, but represents a powerful, angry, destructive, feminine force required to rid the world of evil. Darkness in this representation symbolizes power but not norms of feminine behavior.

Skin-color discrimination is a global social problem (Mire, 2005; Rondilla and Spickard, 2007; Glenn, 2009). It did not originate in Europe and the Americas as a result of European colonial rule, but has a longer local pre-colonial history that has been exacerbated by colonialism and global capitalism. British colonial rule in India reinforced color discrimination against lower caste groups, and now, in the era of globalization, this social problem has resurfaced due to media representations of darker skin as an undesirable attribute. This chapter examines media colorism as a result of globalization of beauty.

Since the mid 1990s, the growth in the domestic beauty, fashion, and cosmetic industries has been directly linked to the successes of many beauty queens in global competitions, who are also Bollywood feminine icons. The **Bollywood** film and cultural industry shapes Indian ideas of feminine beauty and popular youth culture, as well as diasporic Indian cultures in the UK and US, forming a transnational community, and is responsible for reinforcing sexist and racist norms connected to skin color. Bollywood film cultures are also used by UK South Asian communities as a space in which to resist UK cultural racism (Jha, 2006). However, many whitening creams are endorsed by Bollywood film superstars and celebrities, influencing feminine fashions and youth trends and practices. The Indian state and the transnationally mobile business elite deploy the idea of beauty nationalism in Bollywood films and celebrity discourse as an aspect of its **soft power** to construct its success on the world economic stage and seek valorization by US capitalism of its rags-to-riches narrative, which resonates with the American-dream ideology. This chapter begins with a historical context of contemporary India and then explores the ways in which globalization has exacerbated the inequalities of gender, class, and caste by constructing new ideals of Indian middle-class feminine identity, producing stratification based on class, consumerism, colorism, and global mobility. Beauty pageants often highlight societal conflicts of a geographical area and allow us to examine how beauty cultures in these specific locations illuminate conflicting historical power relations between the dominant elite and minority groups struggling to stake a claim on national and indigenous resources. Inequality in India occurs along gender, caste, religion, and class lines, and I investigate the close relationship between upward class mobility and lighter skin/ whiteness as a sign of progress. I examine systematic caste discrimination institutionalized by the dominant upper-caste Brahmin communities and its impact on gender, class, and colorism.

In exploring the globalization of beauty protests, I trace the global travel of the anti-racist philosophy and strategies of Black Is Beautiful to India's Dark Is Beautiful campaign by Women of Worth, and by a grassroots social-media youth organization called Brown n' Proud. Both use feminist media and **cyber activism** to challenge colorism and gender discrimination.

Transnational Feminist Scholarship: Gender and Globalization

Indian feminist scholarship analyzes rather than theorizes the complex lived experiences of Indian women as they analyze discourses of developing and developed, modern, civilized, and Western economic progress in order to highlight the relationship between colonial, postcolonial, and neo-colonial economic and cultural exploitations of Euro-American capitalism. Kumari Jayawardena (1986) has challenged the mythology that feminism is an invention of the West in her pioneering historical research into indigenous feminism in Egypt, Turkey, Iran, India, Sri Lanka, China, Indonesia, Vietnam, Japan, Korea, and the Philippines—and other Third World feminists like Chandra Talpade Mohanty (2003) have voiced concerns about the ethnocentric focus of Western feminism in its assumptions of the universal category of "woman" that erases the differences among women. She asks feminists to practice a contextual analysis by paying close attention to specific histories of colonialism. She also urges Western feminists not to "rescue" **Third World women** (and brown women) and enact the white-savior narrative by depicting them as victims of their cultures. The **white–savior narrative** is a recurring device in cultural representation in which white men and women get to be heroes and rescue people of color from their suffering and oppression. Here, feminine whiteness is valorized at the cost of objectifying women from developing nations as passive.

This chapter uses a transnational feminist approach (Kaplan and Grewal, 1994) by analyzing the interrelated power relations of multiple patriarchies of capitalism, religion, Indian nationalism, and **transnationalism** as social forces shaping women's lives. Transnational feminism challenges the premise of **global feminism**—that women have universal commonality due to their sex—and instead theorizes women as constituted by their local experiences and by their historical and geographical context. It examines the question, "How do global cultural flows promote and reinforce specific national, classed, caste, and gender Indian identities?" Inderpal Grewal, one of the pioneers of this approach, brought to our attention transnational consumption practices of Indian citizens by highlighting the reconfiguration of gender relations due to globalization (2005:26–8). She argues that transnational consumer culture becomes a site of changing and multiple national belongings for Indians, facilitated by new technologies of communication, production, and consumption. In this aspect, the US is not a fixed entity but a dynamic and changing sign produced and circulated in transnational practices of consumption. The formation of Indian **postcolonial identity** is being shaped by the "transnational connectivities of knowledge production" and the neoliberal values of the American dream (rags to riches through individual hard work) embedded in US cultural commodities that Indians consume every day. She analyzed the consumption of the American Barbie doll by middle-class Indian girls—with the Barbie doll's white skin, blond hair, and blue eyes having morphed into a brown-skinned, black-haired, brown-eyed multicultural hybrid Barbie doll, wearing Indian clothes—which, along with an array of US television programs, Hollywood films, and Disney princesses, has shaped their ideas of feminine identity. She suggests that transnational media connections and neoliberal feminine identity integrate a concept of Americanness linked to **cosmopolitanism**, noting that the American South Asian diasporic lifestyle is idealized and followed as an aspiration for most Indians because it symbolizes success (Grewal, 2005:33).

Globalization reconfigures masculine, feminine, sexual, and cultural identities at a personal and intimate level as well as shaping national economic and political structures. It is a contested concept and different academic disciplines define it differently. We can conceptualize globalization as a set of processes and outcomes produced by the coming together of political, economic, cultural, and social factors. The intensification of globalization is due to increased trade and the expansion of capitalism and economic liberalism, aided by improved information and communication technologies linking markets, people, and labor across national boundaries (and virtual space). Global economic institutions such as the **International Monetary Fund**, **World Bank**, and the World Trade Organization control national and transnational economic structures. Arjun Appadurai (1990:301) explains globalization in terms of cultural "disjuncture and dissonance" displaying a complex interrelationship of "people, machinery, money, images and ideas (move across space) ... there have been some disjunctures between the flows of these things, but the sheer speed, scale and volume of each of these flows is now so great that the disjunctures have become central to the politics of global culture." In popular media discourse, globalization is often explained in terms of a threat to a national identity in two opposing frames: cultural homogenization and cultural hybridization.

The threat to Indian culture from Western capitalism can be understood through **cultural homogenization**, also known as the American cultural-imperialism thesis, which holds that Western domination of global mass culture threatens to erase distinct national and local cultures. It highlights the key role of media in the continuing control of cultural institutions of many postcolonial nations. Herbert Schiller (1976), a Marxist scholar, pointed to the crucial role of US media in the global expansion of capitalism, resulting in US cultural dominance. The US and Western European nations use this soft power (Nye, 2005) to gain control over the resources of less powerful countries. Schiller argued that the Euro-American multinationals are supported by their governments in spreading US values through the marketing of Western goods and consumerist culture. This as we have seen, in Inderpal Grewal's analysis, is linked to the global spread of neoliberalism.

The question scholars often ask is, "How do global cultural flows transform local national culture and politics?" In Chapter 1 we used cultural assimilation theory to analyze migrant and minority experiences in the US where migrants feel coerced into (or are driven) to give up their own culture; they acculturate and assimilate into the dominant culture in order to acquire customs and values that allow access to the advantages that the dominant culture affords, particularly upward class mobility. The second frame used to theorize the cultural effect of globalization is **cultural hybridization theory**, which contends that contact between any two cultures inevitably results in mixing, hybridization, and cultural pluralism. This theory explores the ways in which the local culture interacts, domesticates, and harnesses globalizing forces to produce new versions of the local culture and retain a cultural identity. India and many other countries are in this predicament, where people fear cultural assimilation while being aware of the advantages of class mobility of Western cultural assimilation. On the other hand, there is an understanding that culture is always changing and does not stay static, and in this aspect cultural hybridization is beneficial but also presents social problems such as colorism, **sectarianism** as **cultural nativism**, and cultural loss. The concept of colorism was developed in African American and black studies in the US and is connected to the history of European Enlightenment and racism. Radhika Parameswaran (2005) brings attention to a collective stigma directed at dark-skinned people in India by using the work of US-based sociology scholars to define colorism "as a systematic discrimination, historically practiced all over India and integral to the social, institutional and cultural fabric of Indian society." She connects colorism to "skin color discrimination, in which dark-skinned people are seen as inferior, less beautiful, less competent, less intelligent, and less accomplished than light-skinned people" (Gupta, 2012). Also useful is Ronald Hall's (Russell-Cole et al., 2013:2) concept of cosmetic Westernism to understand colorism in a non-Western context. This concept can shed light on the boom in the Indian fairness or skin-lightening cosmetic industry and the discourses of self-transformation that many advertisements convey. Hall connects cosmetic Westernism to economic changes associated with modernization and the transformation of nations from developing to developed. He defines it as "an internalization of psychologically damaging dominant Western beauty ideals by non-Western people and/or by people of color as a consequence of colonial domination" (Russell-Cole et al., 2013:3). He explains it as an assimilation strategy that can only be realized by adapting to dominant cultural expectations. This feeds into is the belief that fair-skin status will permit upward class mobility and **structural assimilation** into a better quality of life. In India, the European racial hierarchy has been enacted through systematic discrimination against lower-caste and indigenous tribal groups.

Historical Context of India

India is the largest democracy in the world, with a population of 1.2 billion, and became an independent nation in 1947 from British colonial rule (1858–1947). India's freedom struggle was decades long. In 1942 Mohandas Karamchand Gandhi launched the mass non-violent civil-disobedience protest known as the **Quit India**

Movement, which was not successful in the short term but eventually resulted in the ejection of British rulers. This movement was supported by the thousands of organizations that made up the All India Congress Committee, including women's organizations, and thousands of Indians were imprisoned for more than three years by the British. The anti-colonial independence movement headed by Gandhi and by the Indian National Congress usurped British colonialism and India emerged as an independent country with an amazing diversity of ethnicities, languages, religions, histories, and traditional customs. Religion was the central force violently partitioning the region into two nations, one for the majority Hindus and one for Muslims in Pakistan. Since independence, India has transitioned from a socialist state-led economy to a capitalist free-market economy (Chandra, 1989).

Jawaharlal Nehru, the first prime minister of India, instituted a **Soviet-style five-year socialist economic plan** to create a secular, democratic, modern nation through massive industrialization. Nehru's economic and political reforms overhauled India's traditional feudalistic and colonial structure. His government instituted poverty reduction, free literacy, and health and welfare programs for the impoverished population living in rural areas. Indian society practices a highly divisive form of inequality—a kind of social apartheid—based on **Hinduism** caste hierarchy of the supremacy of Brahmins and the inferiority of lower-caste groups such as the **Dalits** (a politically self-defined term for lower-caste communities). Bhimrao Ramji Ambedkar (1891–1956) is considered the father of the anti-caste Dalit social movement. Ambedkar and Jyotiba Phule (1827–90) were leaders of an anti-caste social movement who held Brahmins and the British responsible for social discrimination against Dalits. The Indian constitution, designed and written by Ambedkar, criminalized untouchability and caste discrimination, guaranteed equality and freedom from discrimination based on gender, caste, or religion, and instituted reservation policies in employment and education for historically marginalized lower-castes group such as Dalits and outcast tribal groups such as **Adivasis**. Dalits constitute 24.4 percent of India's population and Adivasis 8 percent (Census of India, 2011). According to Ambedkar (1917), **caste organization** is a coercive spatial segregation of groups based on birth, occupational hierarchy, and endogamy (patriarchal rules inhibiting marriage outside of caste groups) to ensure reproductive purity and continuing economic exploitation. Caste was based on the demeaning notion of untouchability, a religiously inflected purity and contamination rule, where people of lower castes were not allowed contact with people of higher castes. This system dehumanized a large group people and condemned them to a degraded and segregated existence due to rituals of untouchability and structural poverty. In 1989, the government fulfilled its post-independence promises of redressing systematic caste discrimination and economic exploitation by implementing the **Mandal Commission** proposal of redistribution of resources through a **positive-discrimination quota system** to challenge caste stratification by increasing reservations of government jobs and public university positions from

27 percent (in the 1960s) to almost 50 percent. However, this redistribution policy faced a backlash with widespread protests by upper-caste college students. Reservation policy became a mobilizing force for the privileged upper-caste elites in the 1990s and resulted in a popular right-wing Hindu revival; and in June 2014, the **Bharatiya Janata Party (BJP)**, a fundamentalist **Hindu nationalist party**, won the national elections.

Dalit political identity consolidated in the face of the Hindu-majority backlash in the late 1980s. The Dalit activist groups sought alternative strategies to challenge systemic structural discrimination by making caste discrimination more visible in an international and global context and comparing it to other brutal social oppressions, such as racism. Casteism, like racism, is a system of economic exploitation, violence, and suffering, and, as such, Dalit activists were recognized by the Third UN World Conference Against Racism, Racial Discrimination, Xenophobia and Related Intolerance (WCAR) held in Durban in 2001, with casteism seen as oppressive as racism in the US and South African apartheid (Reddy, 2005:543).

In 1992, the then prime minister, V. P. Singh, in conversation with the International Monetary Fund and the World Bank, replaced thirty years of state-led socialist economic policies with capitalist free-market economic reforms to address the worsening financial and debt crisis. This opened up the domestic market to global capital and triggered massive privatization of public institutions. The biggest change that has occurred over the last three decades as a result of economic liberalization, including industrialization, urbanization, and globalization, is the expansion of the middle class. India has transitioned from a developing nation to a consumer society, and between 1994 and 2004 it reduced poverty by 8 percent (UN Development Institute); but 37.2 percent of the population still live below the poverty line. Consumption in India is propelled by the expanding middle class, which has the disposable income to buy luxury goods as status symbols, and thus consumerism fuels markets and profits (Jodhka and Prakash, 2011).

There is a contradiction in that India is still a developing Third World country but has emerged as one of the economic powers of the world over the last two decades. India competes with countries like China and Brazil and is included in the BRIC economy, an acronym that refers to Brazil, Russia, India, and China as the four fastest advancing economies—or the "Big 4"—that are predicted to overtake the developed G8 countries (Canada, France, Germany, Italy, Japan, the UK, the US, and the European Union) by 2050, according to Jim O'Neill (2001), a global economist at Goldman Sachs. India's sustained economic growth is attributed to its educational achievement and English proficiency, the development and use of technology of social connectivity, the availability of a large population of highly educated skilled young workers who provide cheap labor, and the rise in the middle-class population, which forms its consumer base. The growth in the service sector means more employment opportunities for the dominant groups in the urban middle classes, including women.

However, India's rising prosperity still does not benefit a very large number of poor people. A McKinsey report on global economic changes (Gupta *et al.*, 2014) shows that India, unlike China, has neglected its public health, education, and infrastructure development. The result is that the vast majority of Indians who do not have surplus income and family wealth cannot access private health care and good education. India is proud of being the largest democracy in the world but systematic labor exploitation and gendered violence are prevalent against lower-caste and tribal groups, and poverty has remained endemic. India has no welfare system (although it does have some state poverty-alleviation programs) so caste hierarchy is closely connected to generational advantages, family inheritance, and social networks (Jodhka and Prakash, 2011).

Fernandes and Heller (2006:495) argue that the rise of the middle class has not resulted in economic democratization for the majority, as even within middle-class jobs women are often paid less than men and are directed to more casual and insecure jobs like secretarial work. The new capitalist economy has benefited upper-caste groups and the women in these groups due to the expansion of private-sector, multinational corporate, and white-collar jobs, whereas poorer groups from lower castes that are much more reliant on state resources and reservations in jobs and university seats have lost out, creating stratification within the middle class. Working-class women's labor is exploited by multinational firms paying lower wages for casual work, and this results in a new division of labor (Jodhka and Prakash, 2011).

Globalization, Gender, and Indian Femininity

Nisha Pahuja's critically acclaimed documentary *The World Before Her* (2010) explores the ways in which globalization and capitalist economic policies have transformed gender relations in Indian society, impacting young women's lives. The documentary focuses on their participation in two very different types of training camp, the Miss India beauty-contest grooming camp organized by *Femina*, a women's magazine, and a militant Hindu-nationalist training camp (called Durga Vahini), organized by **Rashtriya Swayamsevak Sangh (RSS)**. This is a right-wing Hindu-extremist paramilitary organization that has participated in anti-Muslim and anti-Christian violence. In India, beauty contests are understood as sites of Westernization and sexualization but also as opening doors to the American dream, the entry portal to material prosperity and a better standard of living. Beauty contests are seen as offering class mobility to young women, whereas the militant religious training camp aims to inculcate sectarianism and fundamentalist religious ideologies that resist Westernization and sexual immorality and advocate a return to traditional Indian values, defending the Indian family, and the Hindu Nation. In addition, female trainees undertake military and ideological education to defend India's cultural and religious values against the onslaught of Westernization and Islamicization. The portrayal of these two groups of women's lives, participating in camps with opposite extremes of ideology, highlights the ways in which women's bodies have been used to represent the ongoing conflict between tradition and modernity since India's independence.

In globalizing India, middle- and working-class women's labor participation has increased, burdening women with family and work responsibilities and changing family structures. Grewal (1999:799) examined the impact of the economic changes on the construction of Indian femininity. She argued that the "ideal feminine subject" constructed by the media is a "hybrid, cosmopolitan female consumer subject," who is globally mobile, culturally educated in Western styles, proficient in English, emulates western femininity, and at the same time is well versed in patriotic and nationalist duties related to family and home. Leela Fernandes' (2000a:88) ethnographic interviews with middle-class women illuminate the fact that ordinary women have to juggle work, consumerism, and family duties and compare themselves to the ideal femininity represented in these images. In India, like in the US, consumer culture is constructed as a space of feminist empowerment achieved through shopping and consumer literacy. Shoma Munshi (1998:573), a media and cultural-studies scholar investigating gender and advertising, argues that Indian female consumers are constructed as multidimensional and their ideal feminine identity combines the traditional gender roles of mother, wife, and daughter-in-law, as well as a professional career to attain middle-class respectability, thereby constructing a "New Indian Woman." She understands advertisements as sites of both resistance and domination. The advertisements she analyzed offered resistance to traditional female roles as wife, mother, and daughter-in-law by offering consumption as a solution. This notion of ideal femininity as a site of multiple aspirations excludes women from lower classes from consumption and the resources of education, beauty, class, caste, and gender.

Beauty Queens and Indian Nationalism

India and Venezuela have had the highest number of Miss World winners in recent years and, as a result, Indian and Venezuelan women's beauty has been validated by global Eurocentric beauty standards. Beauty queens' global accomplishments are used to augment the success of Indian capitalism in competition with China and Brazil and its expanding soft power on a global stage; they certainly played a part in winning the bid to host the 1996 Miss World pageant. India's success in international beauty contests has resulted in domestic and global expansion of the Indian beauty, fashion, media, and film industries. Parameswaran's (2001) research reveals that, for Indian capitalists, beauty contests are a business opportunity to create markets and brand communities. She explains that the expansion of beauty consumption has resulted in lifestyle changes associated with exercise, slimming, and body modifications, with "increases of 30 to 40 percent in women's memberships in fitness clubs and requests for plastic surgeries have leaped by 20 to 30 percent from 1990 to 1995" (Menon, 1996; Sitaraman, 1996; cited in Parameswaran, 2001:77).

Beauty contests have proliferated all over India, sponsored by multinational and domestic cosmetics, fashion, and consumer industries. International beauty-pageant winners such as Aishwarya Rai (Miss World 1994), Sushmita Sen (Miss Universe 1994), Priyanka Chopra (Miss World 2000), Lara Dutta (Miss Universe 2000), Diana Hayden (Miss World 1997), Yukta Mookhey (Miss World 1999), and Diya Mirza (Miss Asia Pacific 2000) have all entered the Bollywood film industry on the basis of their wins and generated massive individual financial and cultural capital by becoming popular film stars and celebrities (Parameswaran, 2005:420). *Femina*, the women's magazine that organizes the Miss India beauty pageant, is owned by a multinational corporation and targets English-speaking middle-class women, focusing on beauty, fashion, and entertainment. The winner of Miss India competes in the Miss Universe pageant. *Femina* organizes grooming camps for Miss India contestants and for Miss Universe contestants, as depicted in *The World Before Her* discussed above. Susan Runkle (2004:146) conducted her ethnographic research into the 30-day training program of *Femina*'s Miss India pageant by staying with the 23 contestants. She found that the young women (all 5'7" in height and under 25 years of age) were trained daily in a regimented beauty schedule. They were "made beautiful" by fashion, film, and beauty-industry experts in fitness, diet regimes, and beauty tips for competing in international pageants. She explains that this

> gives young women who compete in the pageant the chance to create a social network that will allow them to build careers in the glamour industry... simply being able to make it into the training program can serve as a life changing experience for many young women.
>
> (Runkle 2004:146)

She notes that the beauty pageant provides financial and cultural upward class mobility and opportunities for lower-middle-class women, and leads to considerable success in a variety of other professions. She explains that *Femina*, the women's magazine, portrays its beauty contests as a kind of progressive feminist modernization. This is the same as **consumer feminism** in that it employs feminist themes of empowerment to market products, directing consumerism's focus on individual consumption as a primary source of identity, affirmation, and social connections. For beauty contestants, success opens doors in the media, Bollywood, and the fashion industry.

Feminist scholars such as Ahmed-Ghosh (2003), Runkle (2004), Parameswaran (2004), and Oza (2001) have all analyzed the importance of the 1996 Miss World pageant as a significant global media event where the meanings of national identity were fought over by different groups; and the opposition to the pageant illuminated societal conflicts. Since then, in many developing nations, there have been protests such as the one held in Bangalore in 1996, and in Nigeria in 2002, against the Miss World contests. In 1996, the anti-globalization protests against this global media event included multiple constituencies such as feminist organizations, Marxists, and the right-wing Hindu religious-fundamentalist party, BJP. Huma Ahmed-Ghosh (2003:209) highlights the contradictory ideologies represented in media and beauty advertisements shaping ideal Indian femininity as simultaneously traditional, religious, and modern. She notes that media representation valorizes the traditional Indian woman as virtuous, sacrificing, submissive, and sexually chaste in the idealized roles of "sacrificing mothers and suffering wives" in widely popular TV serials focused on Hindu families. Ahmed-Ghosh highlights a regressive cultural and religious turn, "the trend in recent years of traditionalism based on a revitalized hegemonic Hindu ideology," which coerces women into being "sacrificial, obedient, and devoted wives and mothers." In contrast, the modern woman is represented in the media as "the 'liberated' Indian woman through advertisements and beauty pageants" (Ahmed-Ghosh, 2003:213). In the media, beauty queens are praised for their negotiation of traditional, local, and global cultures to produce a cultural hybridity that is authentically Indian. Rupal Oza (2001:1067) also highlights the dominance of discourses of sexual exposure and modesty at the Miss World protests, specifically targeting the swimwear competition, which was viewed as denigrating to Indian women's honor and respectability by the conservative Hindu nationalist party. Religious groups' desire to protect Indian women's honor from Western values of sexual exposure was constructed in terms of acceptable and unacceptable sexual behavior and morality associated with the social control of the woman's body. Oza (2001:1081) argues that the feminist and Marxist groups were also complicit in focusing on women's bodies and articulated national identity in terms of protecting Indian women from commodification, consumerism, and capitalist exploitation of multinationals.

The Exceptional Neoliberal Femininity of Aishwarya Rai: Transnational Multicultural Mobility

Aishwarya Rai's victory as an international beauty queen highlights the appropriation of female bodies by national discourses. Three themes predominate in Indian media discourses on Aishwarya Rai. The first theme is global and transnational mobility as a discourse of the ideal Indian subject; the second is her massive marketing potential as a Bollywood star; and the third is the approximation of a white aesthetic, displacing dominant Eurocentric beauty standards with a lighter-brown multicultural one. Aishwarya Rai, as a Bollywood film star and celebrity, is also a global brand ambassador of L'Oreal cosmetics (Figure 3.2) who crosses national borders effortlessly and circulates in national and global cinema and media events. She is viewed as the ideal "national–global Indian" subject.

Figure 3.2 Indian beauty advisor Aziza Mistry sets up her L'Oreal Paris cosmetics stand in front of a picture of Aishwarya Rai (left), Pantaloons fashion store, Mumbai, December, 2003

Source: Rob Elliott/AFP/Getty Images.

Beauty queens are national emissaries representing national culture and values, not only in Indian media but also in global media. Their global currency is elaborated in their cultural hybridity. Rai's success created euphoria in the Indian state and media elite class as an example of the rise of Indian capitalism and the success of the free-market ideology of economic globalization. Discourses of exceptionalism are never difficult to find in media talks and conversation.

Parameswaran and Cardoza (2009:229) argues that contemporary standards of ideal beauty are set by beauty queens like Rai, in that representations of femininity in advertising are defined by "fairness, slimness, youthfulness, light skin, long legs, and big eyes," and these beauty standards are propagated by beauty queens, like Rai, whose lighter skin color and approximation of whiteness is idealized as the new requirement to demonstrate consumer modernity and progress in India. It is Rai's bodily attributes of lighter skin and approximation of a white beauty ideal and her Bollywood popular cultural iconicity and status that allows her mobility and circulation in a transnational context. Indian and South Asian women's bodies have irrevocably been transformed to fit Western ideals with help of beauty aids such as skin-bleaching creams, dieting practices, contact lenses, and hair straighteners.

Beauty Inequality: Caste, and Gender Discrimination

On September 28, 2008, *We the People*, a television talk show that has won national awards and is anchored by the popular Barkha Dutt, aired a show called "Why are Indians obsessed with fairness?" on New Delhi Television. Barkha Dutt posed provoking questions to the Indian audience such as, "Is India a country of closeted racists? Even today, are we obsessed with fair skin and are we biased against those with darker complexions? Has globalization created widespread skin-color discrimination or was it integral to Indian culture?" In India, there has been a tradition of privileging fair skin, and there is a legacy of skin-color discrimination against women and lower caste and tribal communities. Dark-skin stigma has been an integral part of Indian culture since pre-colonial times and was reinforced by colonial ideas of superiority associated with whiteness. Skin-color discrimination in India is constituted by a range of unequal intersectional structural power relations such as religious and cultural caste systems, gender, regional, urban, and rural divisions. Varsha Ayyar and Lalit Khandare (2013:71) argue that the values assigned to dark skin are derived from the structural hierarchy founded on caste–color–class hierarchy. They begin their article by foregrounding many cases of racism and racist attacks against African students in cities. They point to the fact that Dalit women face exploitation and a higher burden than upper-caste women due to the fact that lighter skin color is often associated with a higher-caste status. We have discussed that the idealization of whiteness flourishes in media images influencing Indians by the presence of global culture and its embodiment by beauty queens and Bollywood stars. Ayyar and Khandare (2013:86) note that physical characteristics are often coded in caste and class values and extrapolated to moral and behavioral qualities. Indian languages and cultural references are intensely pejorative in "associating darkness with poverty, backwardness, villainy, dirtiness, and impurity, whereas fairness is associated with values of success, prosperity, purity and innocence."

However, it is important to note that in one family there can be a range of skin tones from very light to very dark and therefore in India a binary of white and black skin is not a useful way of understanding structural discrimination, as it is in the US. There is no doubt that popular perceptions and social interactions are shaped by religious and cultural history, but in reality many women and men of dark skin color are also from the upper Brahmin caste, both in South and North India, and it is not as straightforward as understanding dark-skin stigma as a form of caste discrimination and/or class discrimination. Between North and South India, there are regional skin-color differences, and North Indians are often of lighter complexion and South Indians of darker complexion, although there is as wide a variety of skin tones in the South as there is in the North. In everyday interactions, darker skin complexion is negatively associated with lower-caste status due to outdoor manual labor, sun exposure, and resulting skin aging.

Skin-color discrimination in the Indian subcontinent predates the arrival of Mughal rule, European colonialism, and contemporary globalization. There are several contrasting scholarly views on the origin of the caste system in India and thus on the origin of skin-color stigma and its association to caste discrimination in India. One view is that color prejudice originates in the Hindu *varna* system (caste organization and color hierarchy) prevalent in ancient India. Another is the myth of the **Aryan race theory**, in which the upper caste Brahmins saw themselves as having a common descent with the Aryan race, who were the original speakers of Indo-European languages and who were descended from the Caucasians (sharing descent with the same master race as Germans and the British); and yet another is the **orientalist** and colonialist reinforcement of Aryan race theory and caste hierarchy. Scholars disagree about the meaning of *varna* as it has several meanings, ranging from color to classification. Sucheta Mazumdar (1989:49), one of the earliest scholars to investigate South Asian racism in the context of US race politics, explains that sociologists and historians have disputed both the legitimacy of caste as a skin-color-based system of socio-economic classification and the veracity of the Aryan theory of racial conquest. She explains that notable Indian historians such as Romila Thapar have shown that there is no evidence of Aryan invasions and therefore no basis for the Aryan race theory. Brahmins used the theory of common descent to negotiate advantages with European Aryans, as well as justify their dominance in the caste structure against lower castes. The dark- and light-skin regional divide in India may have been sustained by dominant upper-caste groups exploiting the differences between the Aryans of the North and the Dasa (meaning "slave" in Sanskrit) of the South.

Ayyar and Khandare (2013:71) urge us to hold the British and the Brahmin upper caste responsible for colorism and racism, and see skin-color discrimination as a legacy of the Hindu caste system. They argue that the skin-color discrimination practiced in Indian society is pre-colonial and has its origins in the mythical Aryan race theory propagated by the elite upper castes. Darker-skin discrimination and inequality, in their analysis, has always been associated with lower-caste status and socioeconomic positions in India. British colonial rulers reinforced the advantages of the lighter-skin caste-related status of the Brahmins by classifying and dividing the population along caste lines in the development of the first census in India in 1930. This is a very similar situation to the one in the US we examined in Chapter 2, where lighter-skinned mulattoes gained advantage over darker-skinned blacks in upward class mobility. Skin-color prejudice in postcolonial India is linked to the lasting impact of British imperialism and the historical legacy of institutionalized **white supremacy** and internalized racism that colonial rule normalized in Indian culture. Indian class hierarchy is shaped by colonial Western values that the upper classes were acculturated into, through the education system, socializing the upper and middle classes into disdain for the rest of Indians. Poor Indians are often described in newspapers and government reports as backward, uneducated, and uncivilized.

Gender, Caste, Community: The Intersectional Power of Colorism

The higher status attributed to lighter and fairer skin becomes obvious at the birth of a female child in Indian families. Parents and grandparents often comment on dark skin as a misfortune, disadvantage, and disability. This is due to the practice of the marriage dowry system in which girls' parents have to pay for their daughter being accepted into the boy's family. The dowry system, although illegal, is a compulsory Indian custom in most arranged marriages, and is still widely practiced, resulting in families getting rid of female children through feticide. The dowry payment is in cash and includes an array of gifts of gold, jewelry, saris, as well as payment for a house, car, scooter, television set—all depending on the wealth of the families involved. This leads to the devaluation of female children and the valuation of male children. Beauty in Indian culture is inextricably connected to fair skin and large dowries may be demanded from women without education and employment, and women who are considered to be dark or unattractive. A girl's skin tone is seen as a crucial negotiating tool in the dowry system and in the marriage market; the darker the complexion, the higher the dowry. Matrimonial advertisements in newspapers also place a high value on a prospective bride's light-skin color. Ayyar and Khandare pointed to a survey undertaken in 2011 conducted by India's most popular matrimonial website, shaadi. com, that revealed almost 49 percent of men and men's families wanted "fair and wheatish skin-color" brides (Singh, 2011, cited in Ayyar and Kandare, 2013:74).

Amali Philips (2004:253) argues that skin color is a symbolic currency used as leverage in marriage and dowry bargaining, but that the higher status of fair skin is affected by other factors such as caste, class, and community-kinship networks. In her anthropological study of over one hundred Syrian Christian and Latin Catholic households among middle-class Christians in Trivandrum, the capital city of Kerala in South India, she examined the relationship of group identity to femininity and skin color. She reflects on the importance of skin color in "three related areas: in the construction of caste and sub-communal identities; in defining beauty norms and feminine gender identity; and in influencing marriage and dowry negotiations" (Philips, 2004:254). She found that "in dowry transactions 'lighter skin color' and beauty … is symbolically associated with health and moral qualities" and is impacted by class and caste "and kinship connections that enter into marriage and dowry transactions within the Christian middle class" (2004:272).

Media Globalization: Internalized Colorism and Self-hate

Parameswaran and Cardoza's (2007:217–28) extensive research into advertisements highlights the expansion of the skin-lightening cosmetic industry in the last ten years, noting that these advertisements target the growing purchasing power of India's expanding urban and rural female workforce. Fair skin is an asset because it confers many advantages. They found that almost all the models used in advertisements have fairer skin in a country where "most people are varying shades of brown and black" (2007:228). This results in barriers to employment for darker-skin models. Despite this, they note that most women do not desire to be white but an Indian beauty norm which values fair complexion but is not the same as a white beauty norm. They note that this is due to different notions of fairness across different regions, ethnicities, and religions in India (2007:217). This confirms feminist research on how women are influenced more by their peer groups, kinship networks, and local beauty practices in shaping their conception of beauty than by universal beauty ideals. They argue that dark-skin stigma has been reinforced by advertisements and has created self-hate and shame for women. Women with dark skin face employment discrimination, especially jobs in the service industry requiring facial contact, such as receptionists, air hostesses, and TV anchors; and women also suffer by putting themselves at risk by applying harmful chemicals to bleach their skin or by using laser treatments. Fair and Lovely, the most popular skin-whitening product, has beaten the competition from foreign brands and has been sold by Unilever worldwide in 40 countries in Asia, Africa, and the Middle East, with India being the largest single market (Karnani, 2007:4–6). Aneel Karnani (2007), investigating Hindustan Lever Limited (HLL), highlights its strategic marketing to poor rural women by selling its lightening cream very cheaply, in five-rupee sachets (the equivalent of a few cents), and the company's claim that its aim is to democratize access to beauty products for poorer women. He also investigated the efficacy of the cream, finding that there is no scientific evidence that this cream can lighten skin color, not least because it does not contain bleaching agents.

Beauty Protests: Dark is Beautiful

Resistance to colorism has taken different forms, focusing on women's rights, youth mobilization, and social-media activism. In India's vibrant public-media culture, there is increasing discussion of colorism in print, television, and in social media to increase awareness of the problem. Discussions and debates on television programs generate an engaged and critical national audience. Social-media campaigns and cyber activism also generate discussion and grassroots activism at local, regional, and global levels. In 2009, Kavitha Emmanuel's NGO, Women of Worth (WOW), also a feminist organization, launched the Dark is Beautiful public-media campaign as a cultural pushback to counter the widespread valorization of fair skin as having high beauty status. The aim is:

> WOW challenges colorism by trying to sensitize media to redefine beauty standards as well as by drawing attention to the psychological effects on women as a

result of internalized colorism. WOW has been challenging media colorism by initiating discussion on television, identifying ads that are discriminatory, inviting celebrities to be ambassadors for the cause and calling those endorsing skin-whitening products towards responsible advertising. The campaign also appeals to state regulatory bodies to ban advertisements promoting colorism and encourages corporate social responsibility strategies to bring an end to the bias.

(http://womenofworth.in/dark-is-beautiful/)

To celebrate different tones of dark skin, they named the campaign Beauty beyond Color and enlisted the help of Nandita Das, a much celebrated Bollywood film actress, who has a dark skin complexion and who has been discriminated against (Figure 3.3).

Beauty justice campaigns use social media as a way of creating transnational knowledge networks with other anti-colorism (anti-racism) campaigns to highlight the prevalent global problems of skin-color discrimination due to the expansion of multinational beauty companies. WOW was also successful in targeting the Advertising Standards Council of India (ASCI), a governmental regulation organization, to introduce new guidelines for fairness-products advertisements to stop "UNFAIR advertising". They asked their supporters, as viewers and consumers, to report and register complaints with the ASCI about advertisements that promote skin-color discrimination—and they asked them to report brands that practice colorism and to reward brands that celebrate beauty in all skin tones as a way of educating multinationals to practice corporate responsibility and citizenship. Beauty justice campaigns also target high-profile celebrities, such as Shah Rukh Khan, who advertised Fair is Handsome for young men. Shah Rukh Khan is idealized by young audiences and his endorsement was meant to encourage young men from all classes to use lightening creams. This points to a newer trend of targeting working-class and middle-class men by the global and domestic beauty and skin-care industries to expand their markets. WOW's campaign also targets corporations and beauty brands to get them to practice corporate responsibility, celebrate "beauty beyond color" and value dark skin tones. In 2002, HLL responded to the growing public criticism of fairness by launching the new non-profit venture, Fair and Lovely Foundation, to empower "women in India to change their destinies through education, career guidance and skills training" (Fair and Lovely Foundation website, 2006, cited in Parameswaran and Cardoza, 2007:236). The projects of the foundation range from scholarships to fund women's education and free courses for aspiring beauticians to collaborative ventures with state governments and private-sector organizations to train women for careers in garment design and healthcare. This strategy is similar to those used by the Miss America Corporation to counter negative publicity of racism and sexism.

Young people are the most vulnerable to media messages. Brown n' Proud is a youth anti-colorism campaign, based in the city of Bangalore, which aims to create a pride movement that challenges dark-skin stigma among young people in schools, colleges, and

Look anywhere and everywhere, there are blatant and subtle reinforcements that only fair is lovely.

The men have also joined the race with equal number of fairness products.

Such pressure and so little public debate around it!

Stay UNfair.
Stay Beautiful.
-Nandita Das

Figure 3.3 Nandita Das in Women of Worth's Dark Is Beautiful campaign

universities, "by promoting self-pride of darker-skinned individuals who routinely suffer discrimination" (Brown n' Proud, 2014). Their research and survey in the city of Delhi revealed that one in three of a hundred young people aged 18–20 had used skin-bleaching creams and, among 50 school children under the age of eleven, one in four children had used fairness creams and products. They concluded that *rangbhed*, or color discrimination, is a serious social problem in Indian society, and in all South Asian cultures, because it causes psychological damage and inferiority complexes in young people, specifically in young women. Their activism involves legal action and social-media education, as well as community outreach in schools and college campuses, providing workshops and education, and recruiting and training young women and men to challenge inferiority complexes and self-hatred. One of their campaigns challenges the normalization of dark-skin stigma by suing crayon maker Hindustan Pencils, who advertise a flesh-color crayon for children (Figure 3.4). The flesh-colored crayon is peach/beige—definitely not dark brown. Chirayu Jain, a young law student, and one of Brown'n Proud's founder members, was behind the decision to take Hindustan Pencils to court for skin-color discrimination. He explains that their skin-color crayon is a " … a color that neither matched my skin color nor of the majority of people with whom I interact."

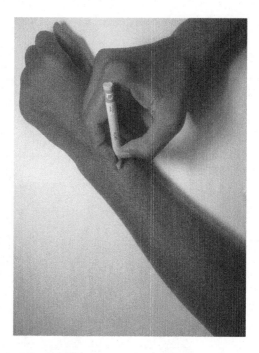

Figure 3.4 Brown n' Proud's Chirayu Jain has drawn attention to Hindustan Pencils' skin-color crayons

Jain believes that everyday practices of language and interactions help to normalize fair skin color and play a "huge role in perpetuating the prejudice against dark-skinned people in a country obsessed with fairness creams ... 'skin' crayon instils in us the idea of the perfect skin color, something that we hanker after for the rest of our lives."

Conclusion

This chapter focused on the expansion of capitalism to India and the resulting whitening of beauty norms affecting Indian women's lives. We explored four key themes: the economic transformation of the Indian nation, the globalization of beauty pageants, the expansion of the middle class resulting in consumer capitalism, and the role of capitalism and media in consolidating skin-color discrimination, creating dark-skin stigma. The chapter highlighted how the globalization of beauty has reinforced gendered, class, and caste inequality in the contemporary valorization of consumerism. We learned that skin-color discrimination as a global problem has been reinforced by globalization in India, exacerbating pre-existing colorism in traditional marriage customs and in the caste–class–color hierarchy.

The gendered nationalism that beauty queens generate in their fans is an aspect of beauty nationalism that gains value by being global, where global is sign of economic progress and Western cultural superiority. The Indian state and media and business elite routinely use beauty queens' success at international beauty pageants to reaffirm free-market ideology and Indian nationalism, and to reaffirm the ideal Indian identity as globally mobile, transnationally connected, English-speaking, and cosmopolitan. Aishwarya Rai represents an exceptional neoliberal femininity by combining her beauty and sexual currency, developed in the Bollywood-film, cosmetic, beauty and fashion industries. I investigated the ways in which transnational beauty cultural flows have promoted and reinforced a new ideal of middle-class identity. The beauty ideal of lighter skin as an asset has created social problems of colorism, sexism, and racism. I illuminated the historical production of beauty inequality based on caste and class stratification by opening up the history of caste–color hierarchy in India to contextualize contemporary formations of media colorism and cosmetic Westernism. I ended the chapter by highlighting the media and cyber activism of two anti-colorism organizations that draw on anti-racist global social movements.

DISCUSSION QUESTIONS

1. How have Indian women's bodies been reconfigured due to economic globalization? How is beauty capitalism implicated in constructing new ideals of Indian middle-class feminine identity? How does beauty consumption create gendered, class, and caste inequality in India?

2. How is beauty used in Indian nationalism and how is it different from the way beauty was used in black nationalism?

3. How is consumption of skin-lightening creams linked to discourses of modernization, Westernization, and progress? How has this exacerbated gender discrimination? What is the local and pre-colonial cultural history of skin-color discrimination in India?

4. How do feminist organizations challenge colorism and gender and caste discrimination?

IV: Chinese Femininity, Beauty Economy, Cosmetic Surgery

꩜

Introduction

Becoming beautiful is everyone's right. It's a very natural desire ... Before, I couldn't imagine that it was possible to have places where the old could become young and the ugly could become beautiful," said Liu Yulan, sixty-two year old contestant.

(Wen, 2013:3–5)

On December 18, 2004, China staged the world's first "Miss Artificial Beauty Pageant" in Beijing, a beauty pageant that required contestants to have undergone plastic surgery, the first of its kind in the world (Figure 4.1). The 19 finalists (aged 17–62 years) included Liu Yulan, the 62-year-old contestant quoted above, and Liu Xiaojing, a 21-year-old transsexual, who was a man until three years ago. She said, "I am now legally a woman and this contest is my first formal step toward womanhood." Both contestants were portrayed as ordinary people who had overcome natural barriers to attain "man-made" beauty by using medical technologies and scientific expertise provided by the cosmetic-surgery industry. Liu Yulan explained that achieving beauty was a matter of individual choice and was empowering for her. However, what she left unsaid was that gendered age discrimination suffered by women of her age group can now be circumvented.

This chapter examines the popularity of cosmetic surgery in China as an integral part of beauty consumer culture. This beauty trend is linked to the economic globalization of China that has produced drastic cultural transformations, restructuring Chinese identity and gender relations. Transnational media, consumer culture, and information networks have added to Chinese women's consumption practices and consumer literacy in neoliberal skills. In the late 1980s China opened its borders to global market capitalism after 30 years (1949–79) of state-planned socialist **Maoism**, and, since then, has transformed into a world power. In 2007, Zhang Zilin, a Chinese actress and a fashion model, became the first Chinese winner of Miss World. Like the international-beauty-pageant winners in India, she has appeared in government

Figure 4.1 Feng Qian beat 18 other contestants to win China's Miss Plastic Surgery, or Miss Artificial Beauty, Beijing, December, 2014

Source: Cancan Chu/Getty Images.

publicity as a cultural ambassador to promote China's image overseas. China's fast-growing cosmetic-surgery industry is linked to beauty pageants' widespread popularity. International beauty pageants promote Eurocentric beauty ideals and perfectionism, contributing to the rise of the cosmetic-surgery industry in conjunction with consumer and popular culture. The Chinese government's neoliberal state policy of the beauty economy has also influenced the popularity of beauty pageants and cosmetic surgery.

Gary Xu and Susan Feiner (2007), two feminist economists, point to the importance of the economy on culture and body norms by analyzing how *meinu jinji*—the state-sponsored beauty economy—shapes female commodification as an aspect of neoliberal capitalism. Susan Brownell's valuable scholarship on reconstruction of Chinese bodies in cosmetic surgery and in sports, shaped by consumption and Chinese nationalism, is important in understanding social changes. She says, "historically in Mao's era, cosmetic surgery was viewed as bourgeois class pathology but it has been repackaged and celebrated as site of consumer freedom, individuality, and human nature" (Brownell 2005:142). Feminist anthropologist Jie Yang's ethnographic research into beauty salons to understand the effects of aging—*nennu to shunu*, from youthfulness to ripe maturity—for women in Chinese male-dominated culture (2011:334) is relevant for any society.

Chinese beauty culture is an aspect of consumer culture shaped by US capitalism embedded in transnational and local cultural flows of global capital. China's economic boom has impacted Chinese women's lives by opening up new forms of modern femininities constructed by the beauty (cosmetic-surgery) industry. Jie Yang (2011) argues that beauty pageants and media advertisements and TV programs have generated a culture of ideal beauty "celebrating the freedom to consume and to invest in one's body aesthetically" resulting in a "cosmetic surgery craze." Yang and other scholars highlight the fact that contemporary media and popular culture are rife with beauty shows, modeling competitions, makeover programs, and stories of celebrities' plastic surgery. They point to the transformation of Chinese culture due to the development of a consumerist ethos where women's bodies are prevalent in advertising, fashion, and mass culture; this has resulted in judging women in terms of what they look like—as beauty objects. Chinese women's bodies are being reconfigured as a result of changing beauty ideals exported by Euro-American beauty pageants and the availability of a range of cosmetics, medical technology, and social trends such as the cosmetic-surgery craze.

In contrast, Lixin Fan's (2011) award-winning documentary *Last Train Home* portrays the life experiences of "the other half," the rural Chinese peasants and farmworkers who make up the huge, cheap workforce of 240 million rural migrant workers creating China's wealth and consumer culture. The documentary takes viewers on the emotional journey of a rural family, separated from their children, who work in urban factories to secure a better future. State-enforced urban residence rules, or the Hukou system, prevent them from settling in the city they work in. They can only go home to their village to see their family for the New Year holiday. The communist government introduced the Hukou system in 1958 as a family-registration system to manage and control the movement of people between urban and rural areas. This system restricts migrant mobility within China and is similar to an internal passport system. It also prevents rural workers from benefiting from the state and private resources of free housing, health, and education available to urban residents. Many scholars writing on this contentious issue understand it in terms of a caste stratification system. Feminist labor scholar activists, Au Loong-Yu and Nan Shan (2007), researching this issue for the feminist non-governmental organization the Committee for Asian Women, explain that the much praised Chinese economic growth has created exploitation in the world's greatest sweatshops and should be understood as social apartheid for the women among the 150 million migrant workers leaving home in search of jobs. They argue this policy keeps wages low for rural migrants. Thus inequality in China is constituted by an intersectional relationship of class, rural residence, and gender discrimination.

This chapter analyzes the impact of economic liberalization and structural reforms on the globalization of beauty in China in the late 1980s. China's economic transformation is reflected in a desire for individual embodied transformation, in a context of massive economic, ideological, national, and cultural transformation. Female bodies and feminine identities are appropriated in shaping capitalist enterprise and in disseminating specific neoliberal techniques of subjectivities to the Chinese population—to socialize the nation in consumer culture. Cosmetic surgery as a national and transnational beauty industry is promoted by the state, and the medical, cosmetic, and beauty industries. China's economic success has created a market for growing numbers of young women in white-collar employment with disposable income to spend on luxuries such as cosmetic surgery; but, as Hua Wen's extensive (2013) ethnographic research confirms, cosmetic surgery is popular in all classes and age groups. Beauty is a form of power and prestige and plays a key role in excluding and/or including different groups of women by distributing advantage and disadvantage, and by blocking and enabling class mobility. This is because it is understood as an economic investment and is understood as a ladder to upward class mobility in an intensively competitive labor market. The Chinese socialist–capitalist state promotes beauty consumption as a way to legitimize its adoption of neoliberal market capitalism. I will examine if this has rolled back the gains made by the socialist feminist agenda of women's equality in Mao's era of state communist rule.

The devaluation of Chinese physical traits—"ethnically correcting" eyes, nose, and height—illuminates the Westernization of Chinese culture. Anthropologist Eugenia Kaw's (1993, 1994:241–65) ethnographic research explains that the popularity of double-eyelid surgery in Asian American communities reflects the aim of achieving a more expressive look associated with Western femininity, embodied in Hollywood female stars. She notes that the racist stereotypes of "looking Asian" connote dullness, passivity, and showing a lack of emotions in one's facial expressions. We will explore if the devaluation of Chinese beauty creates low self-esteem in women and what this might mean for Chinese femininity.

China's cosmetic-surgery craze has travelled from Korean culture via the K-pop phenomenon and the popularity of Korean soap operas. Chinese cosmetic-surgery culture is shaped in interaction with US and Korean popular culture, both widely influential in China. The globally popular **Korean wave (K-wave)**, or *hallyu*, is produced in the geopolitical context of US imperialism, and is understood as an aspect of "globalization from below," challenging the hegemony of US culture even as it mediates Western values and is influenced by black American musical and popular culture. Drawing on scholarship from Chinese and transnational feminist studies, globalization, and Asian American studies, this chapter investigates the cause of the rapid rise of cosmetic surgery in China. In my analysis, the popularity of cosmetic surgery in China is understood as an aspect of cultural assimilation and cosmetic Westernism. In this chapter, I draw from theoretical frames of globalization to understand the impact of colonial capitalism in reconfiguring Chinese women's embodied spaces with neo-colonial discourses of Western beauty ideals. Is this just a case of cultural imperialism where the globally dominant US culture will triumph and Chinese cultural values will be assimilated and become Westernized? Or will Chinese culture absorb specific influences and produce a new hybridized culture? Chinese globalization, like Indian globalization, is paradoxical in that it displays cultural homogenization through economic integration into global capitalism in cultural production and distribution (media, popular culture, and the entertainment industry), as well as the opposite cultural heterogeneity by embodying the fundamental tensions and contradictions of globalization (see Chapter 3).

Historical and Political Context: Situating Chinese Culture

China has transitioned from state-planned **socialism** to socialism with a market economy in the last three decades. Asian American scholar Liu Kang (2004:1–21), investigating Chinese globalization and social changes, argues that China's capitalist economic reform and participation in globalization are explorations of an **alternative modernity**: that is, an alternative model of a consumer society. He examines the two great leaders who have shaped China in last 60 years: Mao Zedong (1893–1976), who is considered the founding father of the People's Republic of China, and Deng Xiaoping (1904–97), who brought in market reforms after Mao died. Globalization in China can be understood by their different ideas of modernization.

The Cultural Revolution

In 1949, Mao Zedong (Figure 4.2) established a republic and a communist state, the People's Republic of China. In 1957, he launched a campaign known as the Great Leap Forward, which aimed to rapidly transform China's economy from an agrarian economy to an industrial one. This led to the deadliest famine in history. In 1966, he initiated the Great Proletarian Cultural Revolution, a program established to remove counter-revolutionary elements from Chinese society. It lasted ten years and was marked by violent class struggle. Although this movement benefited the country's rural development, it also divided the country ideologically between those who

Figure 4.2 Mao Zedong on a renminbi bill
Source: Getty Images.

supported Mao and those who did not. This movement paralyzed the economy and brutally oppressed millions of people. Those who disagreed with the movement were persecuted, imprisoned, tortured, harassed, abused, and murdered (Kang, 2004).

Mao's goal was to create a modern society through industrialization and socialist collective reorganization of Chinese society. Without openings its borders to Western capitalism, by the 1970s Mao had transformed China from a predominantly poor agrarian country to an economically self-sufficient industrialized power. Mao died in 1976, leaving a brutal legacy and an economically paralyzed country. Mao is a contradictory figure, much revered as the father of the nation and criticized for his authoritarian rule. Kang (2004) explains that there is a resurgence of nostalgic attachment to Mao. In the last month, a Mao museum has opened and there are folk songs recycled in popular culture praising his role as a leader who transformed China.

Deng Xiaoping, one of the ruling party's politburo members, implemented economic liberalization policies in 1979. According to Kang (2004), Deng's reforms brought phenomenal prosperity while maintaining an authoritarian state run by the Chinese Communist Party (CCP). Deng's modernization plan of economic determinism and privatization has fully integrated China into the neoliberal capitalist world system and pulled China out of an economic crisis. The poverty rate has been reduced from 85 percent in 1981 to 33.1 percent in 2008 (Shah, 2010). The poverty rate is defined as the number of people living on less than $1.25 a day. However, China has become the factory of the world—a manufacturer and producer of goods— because of the state government's strategy of constituting special areas as autonomous spaces for business and enterprise such as **Township and Village Enterprises (TVE)** and **Special Economic Zones (SEZ)**. These business sites function as autonomous spaces where companies are not regulated by laws on workers' rights to the minimum wage and benefits. As these open areas adopt different preferential policies, they play the dual roles of developing the foreign-oriented economy, generating foreign exchanges through exporting products and importing advanced technologies, and in accelerating inland economic development.

Because of its state-planned market economy, China has the most rapidly rising economy in the world. In 2010, it had the third largest **GDP** in the world, with the world's largest labor force, and is currently acknowledged as the world's second largest economy. In 2010, its economy was growing by 10.3 percent annually, but in 2015 real GDP declined to 6.8 percent (International Monetary Fund, 2015) World Bank, *Data: GBP Growth*. In a bid to become a member of the new world order and also to extend a positive perception of itself on the global stage, China began participating in international institutions by becoming a member of the United Nations in 1971, the World Trade Organization in 2001, and by hosting the Olympics in 2008.

Kang (2004) explains that China still adheres to the one-party state that exercises authoritarian state control. One example of when China's state authoritarianism was challenged was the political crisis of the pro-democracy social protests in Tiananmen

Square in 1989. China's challenge to the global capital world system is also a challenge to Eurocentric definitions of modernity because it offers other developing countries an "alternative vision to capitalist globalization." In this respect, China has nurtured economic ties with many countries in Africa, East Asia, and Latin America, and cultivated considerable respect and influence among Third World developing countries.

Political theorist Martin Jacques (2012) also understands China's economic growth in terms of an alternative modernity. He argues that we need to redefine modernization, not just as product of economic and technical market competition, but as a function of history and culture. He proposes that there are four reasons for China's economic success, all of which have more to do with China's history and culture than its economy. First, he suggests that China is a civilizational state rather than a nation state due to its history, stretching back to more than two thousand years. Because of this history—of conquests, absorption and assimilation—China is a very diverse, decentralized, pluralistic society, even as it is also a highly homogenous ethnic society, of which 94 percent of the population is of Han heritage (Jacques, 2012). Second, he points to the importance of **Confucian values** in shaping the institution of the Chinese family as one of the most important in Chinese culture. Third, Chinese families prioritize education and learning as a Confucian cultural value, which, in his view, is one of the key reasons for China's success. Finally, the relationship of the state and civil society is very different than in the West in that the Chinese state is not viewed as an intruder by the Chinese people but as a benign patriarch, integral to the family whose authority is accepted and unchallenged.

To understand contemporary Chinese culture and identity, we also need to situate China in relation to US capitalism and in the circulation of transnational media that promotes the American dream as an aspiration of neoliberal consumption. China's history includes colonization by Japan, semi-colonization by Britain in the 1830s, what Tani Barlow (1993) calls "port colonialism," where the British colonial administration coerced China to open its coastal ports; for example, the opium trade in Shanghai. The history of North American neoliberal capitalism in the Asian Pacific region, specifically in Japan, Vietnam, and Korea (in the context of Cold War politics), has also played an influential role in exporting beauty pageants, consumer culture, and cosmetic surgery through transnational circuits of mass media, popular culture, Hollywood films, and K-wave (*hallyu*). China's history with many of the countries in the Asia-Pacific region has contributed to its cultural, economic, and political formations.

Most scholars writing on neoliberalism deploy either Marxist or Foucauldian theories. Neoliberalism is defined as a relationship of power and knowledge between the state and its population. Prominent Marxist and geography scholar David Harvey's (2007) scholarship on neoliberal capitalism focuses on China's experiment with neoliberalism. Harvey points out that the difference between Chinese and Western neoliberalism is that the Chinese state has rolled back its governance in regulating

Figure 4.3 Women workers manufacture blue jeans, Congshin textile factory, Xintang, the town which claims to produce 60 percent of the world's jeans and is nicknamed the "the denim jeans center of the world," February, 2012

Source: Lucas Schifres/Getty Images.

capital as well as its provisions for the poor and those most at risk. He argues that China, like the West, is also ignoring the growing disparity between the rich and poor, the urban and the rural, the problems of internal migration, and pollution and ecological issues associated with neoliberal capitalism. He contends that the burden of neoliberalism capitalism falls on the most marginalized and at risk, primarily women from rural and marginalized communities (Figure 4.3).

Asian American scholar Aihwa Ong's (1999, 2006, 2010) scholarship focuses on transnationalism and neoliberal subject formations in the Asia-Pacific countries. She understands neoliberalism as a mechanism for governing populations and suggests two types of power relations: creation of subjects (techniques of subjectivity) and control of subjects (techniques of subjection). She frames neoliberalism as a "malleable technology of governing," which can be deployed by different Asian governing regimes—authoritarian, communist, and democratic—to better engage and compete in the global economy. She examines the agency of **overseas Chinese** transnational subjects who invested in strategies of migration and capital accumulation, finding that they strengthened Chinese nationalism and contributed to the emerging "flexible" capitalism in the Asia-Pacific region. She explains that the creation of a **transnational public sphere** by overseas Chinese has bolstered Chinese nationalism. Additionally, she contrasts the position of privileged Chinese citizens with those working in the SEZs. In these spaces, poor, rural migrant women are denied basic social rights, such as education, medical care, and legal protection (Ong 2010), despite their legal citizenship. This enormously reduces the welfare burden of the socialist Chinese state by granting lower taxes, the free use of land, and other privileges to transnational capital for it to profit from the cheap labor of poor rural Chinese women. This is a retreat from the socialist feminist polices of the CCP, which reduced structural discrimination against poor working-class women. Feminism and feminist activism have been an essential component of the state since 1949, when the CCP came to power and women's equality was incorporated into the national agenda, giving women equal access to work and celebrating them as workers and comrades. Traditionally gendered discriminatory practices were banned, including foot binding and prostitution. Mao made feminism integral to the political and economic agendas of the CCP by promoting gender equality as a legally mandated state law. Xu and Feiner (2007:309) explain that beauty and fashion was stigmatized in Mao's era and was viewed as a decadent activity of the bourgeois class. This devaluation of feminine sexual differences, they argue, was a strategy to maximize the use of female labor. However, the emphasis on women as workers, and as equal comrades, helped in partially freeing women from their roles as mothers and caretakers, allowing them access to employment.

Cosmetic Surgery, Beauty Economy, Chinese Nationalism

On December 6, 2003, the Miss World pageant was held in a beach city called Sanya, in Hainan province in China. The Chinese government's endorsement of beauty pageants was a strategic manoeuvre to increase its positive perception on the international stage (to increase its soft power, constituted by culture and foreign relations) as well as facilitate the entry of global brands and beauty industries. Many multinational, cosmetic-brand corporations from North America, Europe, Korea, and Japan compete with one another to target the much publicized purchasing power of the most populous country on earth. Xu and Feiner (2007:315) traced the history of Western-style beauty pageants to 1946, when Miss Shanghai was staged to raise funds for relief after a flood and to showcase modern Chinese women as sign of colonial modernity. The CCP ended this bourgeois practice in 1949, but beauty pageants reappeared in 1976, secretively on college campuses; but now thousands of beauty contests take place across China with hundreds of millions of viewers. The 2003 Miss World Pageant as a global event regenerated Sanya's local economy, promised a huge growth in its cultural and tourism industry, and generated the largest recorded television audience in the world (Xu and Feiner, 2007:315; Wen, 2013:157). Cities compete to host international beauty pageants to attract multinational investment for urban regeneration. After Sanya's success, China hosted six other major international beauty pageants, including Miss World, Miss Universe, and Miss Tourism. China's cosmetic market is predicted to surpass European countries' because of its population of 1.3 billion citizens with increasing disposable income to spend on luxuries including cosmetics, surgical transformation, and health products. China is the world's eighth largest consumer of cosmetics and the second largest in Asia, after Japan (Godfrey, 2004).

The official Chinese state feminist website, Women of China, reported on the cosmetic craze, and Sun Xi, the editor (Women of China, 2012), discussed the topic at length, pointing to the fact that, in a global survey, the International Society of Aesthetic Plastic Surgery (ISAPS) revealed that there were more than 3.4 million plastic-surgery operations in China between 2009 and 2010. China ranks third in the world behind the US and Brazil for the number of plastic surgeries performed. In 2010, the value of China's plastic-surgery market reached 300 billion yuan (US$48 billion), with the industry employing more than 20 million people. By the end of 2011, mainland China had more than 34,000 cosmetic-surgery institutions, including beauty salons, clinics, comprehensive plastic-surgery departments, and hospitals; and the beauty economy had become the fourth largest by consumption following housing, vehicles, and tourism (Women of China, 2012). But it is Korea, a country with a much smaller population, that has the highest cosmetic surgery per capita, as reported by the International Society of Aesthetic Plastic Surgery, and that attracts medical tourism from China and other Asian countries.

Xu and Feiner (2007:307) explain that the term *meinu jinji* refers exclusively to the beauty pageants and model competitions that are popular in China, linking economy, culture, and gender in a nation-building effort. The official CCP position of beauty pageants as an objectification of women has been drastically revised and reformulated as a local and regional economic-regeneration scheme. The national beauty economy is now an integral part of the socialist market vision spearheaded by the state-authorized feminist organization, the **All-China Women's Federation** (ACWF, also known as Fulian). Thus, China's state feminism promotes the beauty economy as an essential aspect of national economic development by simultaneously highlighting the significance of women's consumption of new femininities as a way to expand consumer markets. It also endorses women's labor in beauty parlours in a bid to lower female unemployment created by the massive lay-off of workers from the crisis of 1978, when state factories and manufacturing were dismantled and turned over to private enterprise.

Neoliberal Femininities and Feminism

Xu and Feiner (2007) argue that through the discourses of beauty economy the state is re-educating and socializing the population with neoliberal consumption skills and prioritizing "the production and consumption of 'female beauty' at the center of the Chinese economy." They give an example of Zhang Xiaomei, an ACWF member, who, by launching a newspaper, *China Beauty and Fashion Daily*, initiated the discourse of beauty economy in the public sphere. This newspaper has become very popular and circulates information about the benefits of the beauty economy, linking it to China's economic prosperity. Zhang Xiaomei's feminist entrepreneurialism and governance skills are routinely lauded in linking gender, economy, and nationalism to everyday practices of beauty (All-China Women's Federation, 2003). In this way, a state-sanctioned beauty economy has become a project of nationalism and feminist empowerment. Feminine beauty is a highly valued commodity in the discourses of the Communist Party's beauty economy. In this discourse, a woman's beautified body can be traded for money, access to jobs, marriage, and social networks. Zhang Xiomei's neoliberal feminism contrasts with the socialist feminism practiced in Mao's era, in which women, as a group, were given equal status as human beings and were impelled to build a nation free of inequalities and discrimination. Communist ideology had condemned emphasis on individual beauty as an attribute of individualism and objectification of women. Current state feminism instead reifies beauty and sexuality, and constructs femininity as a currency and source of capital contributing to the building of a national consumer and labor base.

The risk and danger of cosmetic surgery was highlighted in the death of the young pop star Wang Bei, in 2010 (*The Daily Beast*, 2013). The government has not regulated this private industry. The rapid proliferation of cosmetic-surgery clinics has led many beauty salons to offer surgery, and the process is extremely risky. Recently, China's Ministry of Health banned some risky cosmetic surgeries, but most private clinics for cosmetic surgery remain unregulated. The integration of neoliberal economic policy has meant widespread acceptance of consumer culture, focusing on beauty and body modifications as a significant source of individual economic prosperity. Embedded in this idea is the democratization of beauty—that cosmetic products and surgical interventions are now available at lower costs than before, permitting growing numbers of people to access them. Considering that until recently, many of the beauty advantages were only available to the bourgeois classes, this expansion of capitalism and consumer products allows people from relatively poorer backgrounds to access them.

Beauty as Youthful Femininity

Hua Wen's (2013) ethnographic research conducted in Beijing into cosmetic-surgery culture, focusing on interviews with 58 women from ages 16 to 55, found that cosmetic surgery is less taboo in China than in North America and is popular among diverse groups of women, such as women over 40 and divorced women, who are not considered beautiful due to their age and unmarried status. In China, intense job competition seems to be the main reason given by women for undergoing cosmetic surgery. Female university students who are competing in the national and transnational job markets believe that beauty can supplement their academic success in finding good jobs. Wen notes that youth is particularly cherished in a country where women who remain unmarried after 27 are labelled "leftover women," or "left on the shelf," by the government. Jie Yang (2011:333–57) interviewed 32 beauty-care workers, 25 salon clients, and 14 managers, analyzed media reports, and conducted field work in Chang Ping, Beijing, and Jinan. She analysed the recurring discourse of *nennu to shunu* as a disciplinary gender ideology that capitalizes on femininity and female labor. She argues that *nennu to shunu* is a site for both subject formation and objectification: women become both the consumer and the consumed. The self-improvement discourse imbibed in this transformation from ripe women to tender women necessarily includes the cultural and self-devaluation of women's bodies as objects of consumer improvement to attain normal and/or ideal beauty. The body's natural aging process is rendered as a defect to be "normalized." She concludes that the aim of the beauty economy is to develop consumerism and socialize women into neoliberal consumption by commodifying femininity, sexuality, and beauty. Drawing on Naomi Wolf's (1991) analysis of beauty pageants as sites of normalization of patriarchal power, she argues that the idealization of feminine beauty and sexuality in consumer culture hides male cultural dominance because of "its diffuse and pervasive nature" (2011:347).

Cosmetic surgery is a form of self-management, promoting feminine beauty as a currency to control aging and female futures (Figure 4.4). The transformed and improved new self can be surgically created. As we have seen, the most popular cosmetic procedures are blepharoplasty, commonly known as double-eyelid surgery, which is intended to make the eyes seem rounder; **rhinoplasty** to make the nose narrower and higher; liposuction to make the body slimmer; and breast enlargement, using implants. There have also been cases of leg-lengthening and foot-narrowing surgery reported in many national newspapers. Routinely, beauty experts and celebrities are invited on television makeover programs to teach Chinese women about beauty and its benefits and to domesticate cosmetic surgery as a self-improving technique that can transform women's lives by changing the way they look.

Figure 4.4 Lucy Hao, 24, a jewelry trader, poses with her new nose and double eyelids next to a copy of herself on the cover of *Beijing Weekend*, Beijing, July, 2003. Hao sparked a local media frenzy when she announced that within weeks she would undergo cosmetic surgery 14 times in order to enhance her nose, hairline, eyes, jaws, neck, bottom, breasts, and legs. Hao believes being "pretty" is essential for success in China's society. Her surgery cost USD 50,000

Source: Getty Images.

Cosmetic surgery is not only for the rich and the middle class. For working-class women trying to enter service-industry jobs, cosmetic surgery is seen as a tool for class mobility. Due to the expansion of the service industry, women's physical attractiveness and beauty are considered as advantages and, sometimes, a necessity in the face-to-face exchange of selling products to clients, in public-relation jobs, and in any male-dominated business.

Ageism and Employment Discrimination

Jie Yang's (2011) and Hua Wen's (2013) ethnographic research revealed patterns of gendered discrimination against older women. In Wen's analysis of a 2003 review of job advertisements, women over 30 years of age suffered age discrimination, and 90 percent of the jobs were open only to those younger than them. Between 1993 and 2001, 43 million urban employees were laid off, amounting to a quarter of China's total urban labor force (Yang, 2011:346; Wen 2013:100), and most of the laid-off women had worked for most of their lives so were more likely to be above the age of 30. Wen also found that women were often the first to be laid off and the last to be hired back; and, when applying for jobs, they encountered much more discrimination than men. In 1995, the ACWF, extremely aware of its contradictory market feminism, began networking with numerous women's organizations and set up a national re-employment project for laid-off workers from former state-owned enterprises, most of whom were women. ACWF explained that the beauty economy could help provide jobs and income to millions of women made penniless by the massive 1990s layoffs. The women were re-employed in small businesses, such as beauty and hair salons, and/or retrained to start their own businesses (Xu and Feiner, 2007; Yang 2011). The ACWF website says that the beauty sector created 7.3 million jobs in hairdressing, beauty-product manufacturing, training, and advertising, and that by 2004 this had increased to 14 million jobs. There is a huge market for beauty as there are more than a million beauty parlours catering to the needs of a growing middle class. In the beauty economy, women's participation as consumers and laborers, as well as objects of consumption, is couched in terms of a new form of Chinese nationalism by invoking China's ascendance to a world-power status alongside Mao's socialist collectivism. In the beauty business, private ownership predominates and there is a lack of effective government supervision, with the resulting exploitation including low wages, health risks, no job security, irregular work schedules, and sexual harassment (Yang, 2011). In female-dominated occupations, women are paid far less than in male-dominated ones. Wen (2013) argues that cosmetic surgery provides individual solutions to structural discrimination and the inequalities of sexism, aging, and classism. These individual choices are made available in a consumer culture shaped by a market economy.

Chinese Feminism, Beauty Capitalism, and Patriarchy

Feminist scholars, like Tani Barlow and Lydia Liu, have focused on the rich, heterogeneous traditions of feminisms in China. In charting the history of Chinese feminism, Liu (2013) examined an early twentieth-century Chinese feminist, He-Yin Zhen, who figured centrally in the birth of Chinese feminism. Zhen's 1907 article "On the liberation of sex" focuses on the intersectional relationship among patriarchy, imperialism, capitalism, and gender subjugation as a global historical problem. She examined the patriarchal foundation of capitalist modernity and the ways in which capitalism extends patriarchy, precisely the kind of analysis that is missing from state feminist discourses of the beauty economy. Liu suggests that a narrow definition of feminism about sexuality and rights (the liberal position) was insufficient for He-Yin's framework because of the historical context. In this aspect, her concepts articulated a multidimensionality of gender, class, sex, and history. Jie Yang (2011:344) criticized the ACWF as a state feminist institution, arguing that it failed to provide feminist leadership and did not challenge highly publicized issues of gender exploitation, like low pay in beauty parlours. Xu and Feiner question the problematic essentialized role of the female body, feminine beauty, and youth in developing consumer capitalism in China. They argue that beauty is a significant source of individual economic success, and that China's economic growth has reduced women's economic agency to their beauty, or, more accurately, to their ability to appeal to the male gaze. In this framework, women are essentialized for their sexual difference and a "woman's contribution to the national economy is grounded not in her productive activities, but rather in her ability to meet Western norms of beauty and sexuality." They explain that "what is concealed is where the power of ideal beauty comes from? Beauty ideals are shaped and motivated by the male dominated power hierarchy which is connected to men's pleasure and taste" (Xu and Feiner 2007:346). For women to change their bodies as they age reasserts the cultural dominance of a masculine gaze and highlights the insidiousness of masculine domination. The normalization of cosmetic surgery exacerbates pre-existing class and gender prejudices. Cosmetic surgery is seen as a rational business decision to invest in one's future. Some describe it as empowerment rather than as reinforcing/consolidating cultural and institutional structures that are the real cause of women feeling stress, pain, injury, and alienation.

White Beauty Ideal: Cultural Assimilation and Cosmetic Westernism

White skin has been a symbol of higher-class status in China. As Xu and Feiner argue:

> The enjoyment of feminine beauty plays a key role in the formation of Chinese national identity, which derives from the historical differentiation between the Han ethnicity and the "barbarians" and between the "cultivated" aesthetics of

the Chinese and the "primitive" sensibilities of outsiders (Lydia Liu 2006). When Western "barbarians" invaded China in the middle of the nineteenth century, traditional notions of Chinese national identity were undermined by the barbarians' greater power and technological superiority. At the same time, "their women" (white women now visible, but taboo) began to displace traditional Chinese beauties as objects of desire.

(2007:312)

However, it is important to note that Chinese ideas of ideal beauty incorporate a number of elements drawn from multiple regional, colonial, and national contexts. Contemporary cosmetic-market research provides evidence that Chinese women view white skin as a symbol of beauty. Huiliang Li (2013) explains that whitening creams are one of the most popular beauty products, accounting for 30 percent of the total skin-care market. She also highlights the importance of traditional Chinese medicine (TCM) and ingredients in facial-whitening creams. Her archival research into beauty prescriptions recorded in historic medical references revealed the use of TCMs in more than 25 percent of skin-whitening and skin-lightening products thousands of years ago. This shows that skin-whitening beauty practices are not only a modern fashion (as we also discovered in Chapter 3, focusing on India), but have been part of different local cultures since pre-colonial times, and have now been exacerbated by consumer capitalism.

In this aspect, Chinese beauty ideals are derived from a complex history—and body comportment, facial features, and phenotypic differentiations as a way to establish differences between the ruling classes and the peasant communities (working manually in the fields under the hot sun) was a common practice in China. Darker skin was definitely a marker of lower class position, but whiteness was not the sole criterion for beauty. For example, in researching the global phenomenon of the Modern Girl Barlow *et al.* (2005:270) note that in China "the ideal woman's skin color is compared to congealed ointment, white jade or fresh lychee … healthy radiance of rosy colour always accompanied clear skin as the ideal."

Hua Wen's (2013) ethnographic research provides evidence for the idealization of the Euro-American beauty aesthetic. Schein (1994) also supports the overvaluation and commodification of the white feminine body as a site of modernity and progress in her analysis of wedding customs. Xu and Feiner (2007:320) have also added to this scholarship, arguing that there is no doubt beauty pageants promote Anglo-European beauty norms in consumer choice. They chart the changes in the Chinese concept of beauty through to contemporary beauty ideals centering on the admiration and imitation of whiteness, a contempt for one's own cultural and ethnic heritage, and discrimination against those who look "native." Has the integration of China's economy resulted in a devaluation of Chinese ideas of beauty and femininity while promoting a culture of imitating Western beauty ideals? These scholars argue that it is the availability of technological surgical modifications marketed by the medical and cosmetic industries in constructing racial features as defects that has sparked the cosmetic-surgery craze. By reinforcing Chinese women's feelings of devaluation—turning their biology, such as eyes and nose, into a cultural problem—these industries work in tandem with those of beauty, fashion, and media to bolster consumption, creating a thriving cosmetic-surgery market.

One of the earliest pieces of scholarship discussing double-eyelid surgery in North America was conducted by Eugena Kaw (1993, 1994:241–65), who interviewed 11 Asian American women (with origins in Seoul, Beijing, and Taipei) residing in the San Francisco Bay, nine of whom had had blepharoplasty and two rhinoplasty. In the context of the dominance of race in North American life, Kaw argued that ethnic cosmetic surgery constituted a body practice that adds to the racism and cultural and structural inequalities faced by these women, resulting in embodied assimilation. Asian American women felt they had to conceal the more obvious forms of their ethnicity in order not to stand out and be targeted for racist stereotypes. In this way, they reinforced the undesirability of "stereotypical" Asian facial features as "not beautiful." She highlighted cosmetic surgery as site of feminine complicity as women conform to patriarchal definitions of femininity and Caucasian standards of beauty. Kaw concluded that surgery for nose bridges and double eyelids are influenced by gender and racial stereotypes promulgated by institutional and cultural structures of racism and sexism. However, interviewees in Wen's and Kaw's research understood it as individual choice and aesthetic preference that can help them get a date, a better job, and friends. In much of the ethnographic scholarship, women explain cosmetic-surgery consumption in economic and aspirational terms. Kaw pointed out that cosmetic surgery is used by Asian women to improve their class and racial positions and enable them to **racially pass**.

In contrast to the whitening/Westernization thesis of Chinese culture, which constructs women as passive recipients of culture, Sharon Heijin Lee's (2012) doctoral research into Korean cosmetic-surgery beauty practices uses a transnational feminist framework to understand the complex reasons behind the widespread popularity of cosmetic surgery in China, which includes understanding the importance of Korean popular culture, not only in China, but in the Asia-Pacific rim. She understands beauty to be a product of a complex power formation that combines historical, cultural, and geographical contexts that normalize cosmetic surgery in Korea. She questions the anti-Asian racist representations of the US media, which pathologizes Korean women. She argues that mapping "US notions of race onto the South Korean context elides the geopolitical specificities that shape women's corporeal choices by centering the US nation state and further reinforcing the First World/Third World hierarchies that inform US empire (2012)."

Conclusion

This chapter set out to situate the popularity of cosmetic surgery in China's historical, economic, and cultural contexts. I identified four reasons for social acceptance of cosmetic surgery. First, the Chinese experiment with neoliberal economic policies and its participation in transnational consumer culture has resulted in the transformation of Chinese culture. Second, beauty, sexuality, and femininity are constructed as crucial components of neoliberal feminine subjectivity—as individual advantages to be exploited. Contemporary state feminism with the aim of national economic growth re-establishes the "feminine" solely as a site of feminine beauty and sexuality and consolidates femininity as a commodity to develop China's neoliberal economy. Most pertinent to our analysis of beauty and cosmetic surgery is the construction of beauty as an embodied currency and a form of capital (in conjunction with private property, education, and professional skills). Individual women weigh cosmetic-surgery risks in term of economic investment in a future and in their ability to compete in the labor and marriage market. The government's beauty-economy strategy is disseminated through newspapers, television, and social media as a feminist strategy of empowerment and equality. Third, the drastic economic reforms of the last two decades have had uneven benefits for the Chinese population. Some scholars argue that overall the economic reforms have benefited large segments of the Chinese population, while others have shown the growing disparity of wealth and lack of human rights and a "good life" for millions of displaced rural citizens. Women from minority rural communities are disproportionately affected as they migrate, leaving family behind to search for work in the SEZs situated in larger cities. The SEZs are protected by the socialist state in a bid to attract foreign business to the nation. State feminism and socialism are a far cry from the policy of equality in the Maoist era, when socialist ideas of feminism propagated equality in the workplace and access to political governance in public spaces and in the family. The socialist neoliberal feminism of today ignores the gender exploitation of large groups of marginalized women, specifically regarding low pay and insecure employment in the beauty industry, and instead focuses on individual consumer feminist empowerment.

DISCUSSION QUESTIONS

1. How has China's economic transformation resulted in the consumption of cosmetic surgery as a way to increase individual women's beauty advantages? How has beauty become a symbol of economic growth?
2. By exploring China's historical and geopolitical context, how do you understand the nature of subject formation in contemporary transnational consumer capitalism?
3. What is the role of the state's beauty economy in promulgating neoliberal feminism? How has socialist feminism transitioned to neoliberal market feminism? Compare the different kinds of neoliberalism we have examined in Chapters 1 to 3.
4. Can you identify three differences in the conceptualization of the idealized female body and techniques of subjectivities in the medical, cosmetic, and beauty industries?

V: A Complex Model of Beauty

～～×～～

Beauty ideals control, restrict, and discipline women's bodies, desires, and social realities. As Naomi Wolf, analyzing the social fiction of the beauty myth, explains:

> The contemporary ravages of the beauty backlash are destroying women physically and depleting us psychologically. If we are to free ourselves from the dead weight that has once again been made out of femaleness, it is not ballots or lobbyists, or placards that women will need first, it is a new way to see.
>
> (Wolf, 1991:15)

The feminist theories analyzed in this book offer a complex relational analysis of beauty as a site of production of femininity situated in an interaction of multidimensional power relations. For example, Susan Bordo (2003) and Sandra Bartky (1990), in Chapter 1, demonstrated the power of the **global beauty industry** in symbiosis with media and the advertising industry in creating a culture of inadequacy and self-hatred under the guise of self-improvement for women. Beauty is a site of identification, desire, and pleasure. Paradoxically, it is also a site of racial, sexual and class exclusion, shame, and psychological damage. From our analysis so far, we can conclude that beauty's emotional and affective force is important for how female bodies—like that of Nina Davuluri, Miss America winner, as discussed in Chapter 1; Beyoncé Knowles as a global music and feminine icon, as discussed in Chapter 2; and Aishwarya Rai as a Bollywood superstar and former Miss World, in Chapter 3—can become exceptional national and global symbols—as corporate brands. For black women, a cultural space of self-love created by participating in beauty struggles for the Black Is Beautiful movement is always negotiating internalized colorism and externalized racism. In India, lighter skin is a sign of middle-class status. In China, the cultural normalization of cosmetic surgery is linked to the popularity of Korean pop stars and Chinese beauty queens in an idealization of Caucasian feminine body and facial features. A modern feminine body in China signals economic prosperity by assimilating Western consumer habits.

For many women, beauty is also a site of deep emotional connection with women idols and with other women in everyday media practice. Lauren Berlant (2008) argues that "women's cultures" are intimate public cultures, where emotional connection is important in order for women to participate in the public sphere of commodity capitalism, where democratic participation takes place through consumer citizenship. Beauty's affective capacity in popular culture, such as viewing the Miss America beauty pageant, or engaging with Bollywood films, or Korean pop music, arouses multiple affiliations and sexual desires. Beauty and sexuality, as embodied and material assets, are converted into capital and thereby influence the life chances and opportunities of individuals. To understand women's agency, feminist post-colonial theorists and transnational feminists have devised ways of approaching the analysis of beauty as an experience that women take part in, and which situates them in networks of power whereby they produce their subjectivities.

Vanita Reddy (2011:29) uses an intersectional and transnational framework to conceive of a "**beauty assemblage**" that combines the affective aspects of a subject's desires and the aspirations they attach to beauty. In this framework, beauty is an uneven socializing force circulating in transnational cultural flows that can be oppressive and objectify, racialize, and exoticize women; or it can open up small spaces of agency in women's everyday encounters with the world. This concept of the "beauty assemblage" borrows from feminist theories of lived experiences, situated in the beauty struggles that women experience. It offers a complex model of agency because of the contradictory nature of our experiences, shaped by multiple power configurations, simultaneously being objectified and taking pleasure in the embodiment and practices of beauty. This understanding of women of color's experiences invokes the feminist legacies of Cherrie Moraga and Gloria E. Anzaldúa's (1981) *Theory in the Flesh* and Chela Sandoval's (1991) *A Theory of Oppositional Consciousness*, both written from the perspectives of US feminists of color and Third World feminism. Cherrie Moraga and Gloria Anzaldúa's anthology *This Bridge Called My Back* is a foundational feminist text on Chicana feminism in which Moraga compares her pain at silencing her lesbian identity to poverty experienced by her mother, who faced multiple discriminations due to her lack of education as an uneducated poor woman of color of Mexican and *mestizo* origin. Moraga utilized her lived experiences of multiple and intersecting identities as a cultural resource for constituting her feminist consciousness (Moraga, 1983). Her "theories in flesh" then give rise to a practical and oppositional consciousness in the many feminist, Chicana, and lesbian organizations she was actively involved in, challenging the silencing and assimilation she encountered. Her theory in the flesh incorporates these experiences, "where the physical realities of our lives—our skin color, the land or street we grew up on, our sexual longings—all fuse to create a politics born out of necessity;" and she advises that we "attempt to bridge the contradictions in our experience" by building coalitions across difficult differences and by "naming our selves and by telling our stories in our own words" (Moraga, 1983:52–3).

Similarly, Sandoval has called the self-reflexivity required to respond to different configurations of power in women of color and Third World women's experiences "differential and oppositional consciousness." If we apply her conceptualization to the experiences of beauty and femininity, we can see that women of color balance multiple intersections of power relations (familial, local, visual, national, global, and others). Sandoval proposes that a new kind of consciousness is produced through these experiences that allow US Third World women of color flexibility, reflexivity, and knowledge in building a new kind of feminist consciousness available to all women; "differential consciousness permits the practitioner to choose tactical position" (Sandoval, 1991:15). Beauty creates affects such as desire, identification, shame, alienation, cynicism, and ambivalence. It also creates capacities and consciousness that open individual women as subjects to articulations of belonging, caught up in micro- and macro-structural power relations of domination, pleasure, sexual attraction, self-surveillance, privilege, and complicity.

Beauty pageants are platforms for global beauty corporations to create new markets, but, paradoxically, they are also deployed by anti-globalization protests to challenge state and elite control of a society. By analyzing the feminist protests at the Miss America pageant, the Black Is Beautiful social movement, the popular consumer trends of skin-lightening and cosmetic surgery, and feminist, anti-racist and anti-colorism protests, this book deployed beauty as an analytical tool to analyze gendered, classed, and racialized practices to understand the complexity of beauty as a site of social oppression, injury, and social control, as well as a site of resistance to gender oppression.

Glossary

The **abolitionist movement** demanded the immediate emancipation of all slaves and an end to racial discrimination and segregation.

Adivasi refers to indigenous groups of varied ethnic and tribal minorities living in isolated hills, forests, and mountains in India. Adivasis are considered the original native population of India. The Indian constitution designates Scheduled Tribes (STs) as an "at risk" group because of their high levels of poverty and low literacy rates, and grants them access to reservation quotas in government jobs and education.

Afrocentrism refers to ideas and culture that promote African ancestry, history, and the contributions of Africans to challenge the racism of Euro-American knowledge formation. Afrocentrism evolved out of black activists and intellectuals of the US Civil Rights Movement working with the Pan-African Congress.

The **All-China Women's Federation** (ACWF, also known as Fulian) is the state feminist organization. It uses its website, womenofchina.cn, to communicate the state's feminist policies.

Alternative modernity refers to different forms of modernity that have emerged in non-Western contexts, and challenges the Eurocentric idea that modernity was an invention of Euro-American societies.

The **American dream** refers to the ideals of freedom, equality, and opportunity apparently available to every American despite a poor origin. It signifies that a life of personal happiness and material comfort is available to all, including poor immigrants moving to the US with very few resources.

American exceptionalism refers to the idea that the US views itself a special and unique nation—a free nation based on democratic ideals, individual freedom, wealth, and capitalism.

American imperialism refers to the dominance and expanding rule of the US, or American empire, across the world in economic, military, and cultural spheres through the ideology of free-market capitalism. American imperialism is often compared with the colonial domination and expansion of the British Empire of the seventeenth to nineteenth centuries.

Anti-black racism is an institutional and cultural racism that continues to target and exclude people of African descent. It has its historical roots in slavery and the Reconstruction/Post-Reconstruction Era.

Aryan race theory espouses the superiority of the Aryan race over all other races. The Aryans were thought to descend from the original speakers of the Indo-European languages, who were a subgroup of the Caucasian race. The concept of the Aryan race has been used by racists and white supremacists as in doctrines of Nazism and neo-Nazism.

Asian model minority is a stereotype of Asian Americans as academically and economically successful in comparison to other racial minority groups because of their supposedly unique cultural values that emphasize hard work and strong family values.

Beauty assemblage is a collection or gathering of social forces—gender, class, race, nationalism, colonialism—that shape ideas of beauty.

Beauty capital is a concept derived from Naomi's Wolf *The Beauty Myth* (1991), where beauty is a resource and capital exchanged for other commodities fought over in a patriarchal culture.

The **Bharatiya Janata Party (BJP)** is the conservative religious party elected to rule India in June 2014. It is closely associated with a group of organizations that advocate *Hindutva*, a kind of religious Hindu fundamentalism. The affiliated organizations refer to themselves as the Sangh Parivar, or family of associations, and include the Rashtriya Swayamsevak Sangh.

Black Liberation Movement refers to a wide range of grassroots movements that worked for the freedom of black people, such as the Student Non-violent Coordinating Committee (SNCC), the Black Panther Party, the Revolutionary Action Movement (RAM), and the Civil Rights and Black Liberation movements.

Black nationalism is an ideology of unity and self-determination of black people.

Blepharoplasty is the surgical repair or reconstruction of an eyelid.

Bollywood is an Indian film and cultural industry located in the city of Mumbai, or Bombay as it was known. It is also known as Hindi Cinema. Bollywood produces about a thousand films a year, includes India's largest film producers, and is differentiated from other Indian cinema industries such as Tamil-language cinema, Tollywood, Bengali-language cinema, and Assamese.

British colonialism was the racial and economic ideology of the British empire in the nineteenth and early twentieth centuries. See Colonialism.

Capitalism is an economic system of free-market ideology believing in competition and profit. It is an economic and political system in which a country's trade and industry are controlled by private owners for profit, rather than by the state. It became the dominant global economic system due to American imperialism, in turn intensifying processes of economic and cultural globalization. There are four types of capitalism: market-led, state-led, corporate, and social democratic.

Caste organization refers to a stratification system based on a Hindu system of hereditary, endogamous, class structure that is determined by birth and that eliminates social mobility. There are four castes: the Brahmin, Kshatriya, Vaisya, and Sudra castes. Brahmins are the dominant caste.

Caste stratification is a hierarchy based on caste discrimination.

Civil Rights discourses of racial equality and opportunity were a result of the Civil Rights Movement, which was a mass popular movement to challenge racial oppression and to secure access to US citizenship and basic privileges and rights for African Americans. Although the roots of the movement go back to the nineteenth century, it peaked in the 1950s and 1960s. This movement transformed US society and brought equality to minority groups.

Civil society refers to the public space in which citizens come together to create organizations to voice their needs. Includes non-governmental organizations (NGOs) and institutions as well as the family and the private sphere.

Colonialism is the control of one nation by another nation. It involves a powerful nation exerting control over another nation's territory, resources and economy, political structure, and culture. The European colonial period was the era from the sixteenth century to the mid twentieth century. Portugal, Spain, Britain, the Netherlands, Russia, and France established colonies in Asia, Africa, and the Americas.

Color-blind racial ideology focuses on individual achievements of racialised groups to claim that racism is over and hides institutional racism. It is the belief that racism and race privilege no longer exist and therefore race-based affirmative action should be abolished.

Colorism is prejudice or discrimination against individuals with a dark skin tone, typically among people of the same ethnic or racial group.

The **Combahee River Collective** was a black feminist group formed in 1974, which produced an analysis of the interlocking nature of systems of oppression on black women's lives. Its members were committed to active struggle against the racial, sexual, heterosexual, and class oppression that all women of color face.

Commodification in Marxist theory is the transformation of entities such as femininity, education, and beauty that are not understood as goods for sale into commodities that can be exchanged and marketed for a valuable position or status.

Commodity capitalism refers to a consumer society where consumer demand is manipulated, in a deliberate and coordinated way, through mass-marketing techniques, to the advantage of capitalist markets and sellers.

Confucian values are at the heart of Confucianism, a belief system developed from the teachings of the Chinese philosopher Confucius (551–479 BCE). They are religious, intellectual, and scholarly values that teach how to live a moral and just life, valuing education, statesmanship, love for humanity, ancestor worship, reverence for parents, and harmony in thought and conduct.

Consumer feminism refers to gendered practices such as fashion, beauty, and cosmetic surgery resulting from the interaction of consumer capitalism and feminism, where feminist emancipation is understood as having the "freedom" to buy and acquire certain goods and the "choice" to engage in certain cultural and commercial practices.

Consumerism is a belief system that puts a high value on possession of goods, usually as a result of engagement with media culture and the persuasion tactics of advertisements.

Contemporary consumer culture is the dominant cultural activity of today, i.e. the consumption of objects, goods, and commodities. In modern societies the way we live our lives is structured by money, market relations, and economic forces. Individuals attain status and prestige by possessing personal property. Don Slater (1997) challenges the conventional notion that consumption is a trivial activity and explains that consumer culture reveals the ways in which relations of production and consumption mediate each other. Celia Lury (1996) points out the powerful role consumption plays in our lives, creating new social and political identities. See Transnational consumer culture.

Corporate branding Corporations are business organizations authorized to act as a single entity (legally, a person). Corporate branding promotes a product by attaching it to a high-status celebrity or a well-established company name.

Cosmetic whitening refers to internalized racism held by people around the world, because of colonialism and imperialism, that being lighter-skinned and more Western-looking is better and a sign of progress.

Cosmopolitanism refers to an identity (or a way of being) that is at ease in many different countries and cultures.

Cultural assimilation is the process by which members of an ethnic minority group lose cultural characteristics such as language and religious ideas that distinguish them from the dominant cultural group.

Cultural feminism developed from radical feminism—and, although there are differences between them, both shore up women's culture as a site of feminist solidarity. Cultural feminism emphasizes the specialness of women's biological differences— an ideology of superior feminine attributes and behavior arising from women's reproductive capacity.

Cultural homogenization is the characteristics of cultural globalization, referring to the blending of local cultural practices into the dominant culture and resulting in the loss of local cultural habits and a reduction in cultural diversity.

Cultural hybridity or **heterogeneity** is a characteristic of cultural globalization, where the interaction between two cultures creates a new, fused cultural form.

Cultural nativism is the policy of protecting the interests of native-born or established inhabitants against those of immigrants—or emphasizing traditional or local customs in opposition to outside influences.

Cultures of Poverty, or **cultural pathologies**, refers to a culture's behavioral problems. It is often used by conservatives to blame cultures for their poverty. The culture of poverty is a blame-the-victim conservative political campaign to rationalize poverty as an unchangeable aspect of cultures of poor people. The structures of inequality are ignored by explaining poverty as an aspect of culture rather than understanding it as relationship between "structural" and "cultural."

Cyber activism is internet activism, or electronic advocacy, and includes Twitter, Facebook, and YouTube, to create global and transnational communication and networks for fundraising, community building, lobbying, and organizing.

Dalit political identity or the **anti-caste Dalit social movement**. Dalit is a name for historically disadvantaged communities and groups that were regarded as untouchable in the Indian caste system.

Decolonization was the freeing of dependent colonies from colonial rule by establishing political or economic independence and removing the colonizers' rule, culture, and ideas.

Diasporic Indians/non-resident Indians/overseas Indians. A non-resident Indian (NRI) is someone who holds an Indian passport and has temporarily emigrated to another country for six months or more. Overseas Indians refers to people settled in other countries with Indian ancestry. India has the second largest diaspora in the world after China.

Diasporic media spaces A diaspora is a scattering of migrants or groups of people from their homeland who settle in a new geographical location. Diasporic media space refers to alternative public spaces created by diasporas' regular use of media (such as print, radio, television, and the internet) to form imaginary communities in their new locations based on the cultural practices of their homelands.

Economic liberalization is a free-market ideology, derived from liberalism, which results in individual freedom, privatization, and a reduction of the regulating powers of the state. Neoliberalism is an integral aspect of economic liberalization. Its resurgence began in the 1970s and 1980s, endorsed by the conservative politics of US President Reagan and UK Prime Minister Thatcher.

Enlightenment philosophy was a European intellectual movement of the eighteenth century. It was a transformative era of reason, science, education, individualism, and criticism of idealization of religion. The French Revolution in 1789 was influenced by this philosophy.

Eugenicist policy refers to prevalent racial thinking in the eighteenth and nineteenth centuries that, in association with scientific racism, advocated the improvement of the "superior" European races, under the guise of improving the human species, by preventing sexual reproduction with biologically inferior races.

Fair-skin status refers to the advantages of lighter skin in India.

False consciousness is a concept used in Marxist theory and refers to people's inability to see their own exploitation, oppression, and social relations.

Feminism, First-wave focused mainly on suffrage and overturning legal obstacles to gender equality (i.e. voting rights, property rights).

Feminism, Second-wave is a period of feminist activity that began in the early 1960s as a middle-class women's movement in the US, and then became a worldwide movement, fighting on a wide range of issues such as sexuality, family, the workplace, reproductive rights, de facto inequalities, and official legal inequalities.

Feminism, Third-wave began in the 1990s and challenged second-wave feminism's essentialist definitions of femininity. It combines many different types of feminism, rather than privileging the experiences of upper- and middle-class white women.

Feminist consumerism is a corporate strategy that employs feminist themes of empowerment to market products, that shares consumerism's focus on individual consumption as a primary source of identity, affirmation, and social change, and that reformulates feminism as achieved principally through grooming and shopping.

First-wave feminism. See Feminism, First-wave.

Foucauldian analysis, based on the theories of French philosopher Michel Foucault, refers to discourse analysis focusing on power relationships in society as expressed through language and practices.

GDP Gross Domestic Product (GDP) is the monetary value of all the finished goods and services produced within a country's borders in a specific time period (though GDP is usually calculated on an annual basis). GDP is like a price tag on a country's output, and it measures the size of the economy.

Gendered socialization is the process of learning social roles, norms, values, behavior, and social skills and attitudes associated with one's gender shaped by patriarchy. Occurs through the family, parental attitudes, schools, how peers interact with each other, and mass media.

The **global beauty industry** includes skin care, color cosmetics, hair care, fragrances, oral care, bath and shower, deodorant, and other grooming products. It also includes the fashion–beauty complex of media, advertising, fashion, beauty pageants, and cosmetic surgery.

Global feminism argues that women all over the world have their sex in common and are oppressed because of their gender. It has been criticized for universalizing the concept of woman.

Governmental neoliberalism is a new mode of statecraft in which market rationales are embodied by self-regulating and self-governing subjects.

The **Great Migration** was the migration and relocation of more than 6 million African Americans from the rural South to the cities of the North, Midwest and West, fleeing racism, unemployment, and segregation, in 1910–30 and 1940–70.

The **Harlem Renaissance** was a cultural urban movement centered on New York from 1918 to the 1930s that included writers Langston Hughes and Richard

Wright, jazz musicians, singers and dancers like Josephine Baker, and sculptors and painters who addressed racism through their art.

Heteronormative assumptions in mainstream culture discriminate against sexual minorities by privileging monogamous heterosexual practices as normal and natural in contrast to 'deviant' lesbian and gay, bisexual, transgender (LGBTQ) sexual practices. The stigmatization and discrimination takes place routinely in the institution of marriage, tax codes, and employment for LGBTQ communities, and also in the lived experiences of racial minorities.

Hinduism is the religion practiced by the majority of Indians.

Hindu nationalist party. See Bharatiya Janata Party.

Human-capital theory stresses the significance of education and training as the key to participation in the new global economy. It is a key determinant of national economic performance. It is a theory of individual achievement and capacity, often used as a propaganda tool by Conservative right parties against the poor.

Individualism, linked to liberalism and neoliberalism, argues for the rights of the individual over state and collective power. It is the valuing of an individual's self-interest, rather than collective effort and responsibility, as the best way to serve societal and public good.

Institutional racism is any system of inequality based on race, occurring in institutions such as governmental organizations, schools, banks, courts, private business, and the media, and does not necessarily involve intentional racial discrimination.

Internal colonialism is a form of exploitation by dominant groups over minority ethnic groups. It is historically prevalent in the US and contrasts immigrants who came to the US out of choice with those already in the US or brought to the US forcefully, such as Native Americans, native Mexicans, and descendants of African slaves.

The **International Monetary Fund (IMF)** is a financial institution established in 1945 to promote international trade by increasing the exchange stability of the major currencies.

Intersectionality is the study of interconnected relations of multiple forms or systems of oppression, domination or discrimination, first proposed by the black feminist Kimberlé Crenshaw in 1989.

The **Korean wave (K-wave)**, or *hallyu*, refers to South Korean cultural production and includes Korean pop (K-pop) music videos and dramas. It has been globally popular since the late 1990s among teenagers, young adults, and women in many countries. It sets the norms of fashion, beauty, and music in Asia and in diasporic Asian communities.

Liberal feminism, which originated in **liberalism**, promotes gender equality, equal access to education, equal pay, ending sex segregation, and better working conditions.

Liberalism is a political philosophy with the core concepts of individualism, equality, freedom, democratic elections, civil rights, freedom of the press, freedom of religion, free trade, and private property. It was formed in opposition to and by rejecting the ideas of monarchy, hereditary privilege, state religion, absolute monarchy, and the Divine Right of Kings.

Liberal multiculturalism is a political policy that focuses on accommodation to cultural and religious differences of minorities and promotes the institutionalization of cultural diversity. This is often contrasted to other settlement policies such as social integration, cultural assimilation, and racial segregation.

The **Mandal Commission** was an Indian government commission established in 1979, and headed by Indian parliamentarian B. P. Mandal, to redress caste and tribal discrimination using social, economic, and educational indicators to determine the needs of communities.

Manifest Destiny was a widely held belief in the nineteenth-century US that American settlers were destined to expand throughout the continent. The newspaper editor John O'Sullivan coined the term in 1845. John Gast's painting *American Progress* is an allegorical representation of the modernization of the new west.

Maoism is a political theory derived from the teachings of the Chinese political leader Mao Zedong (1893–1976).

Media moral panics are moral crises or controversies created by the media. Moral panics are taboo or controversial issues causing social tension. The media often manipulate issues such as immigration, youth culture, and sexual behavior for political and economic purposes.

Mestizaje refers to racially mixed identity and is prevalent in many countries in South and Latin America.

Miscegenation is interracial sexual relations.

The **Miss America Beauty Pageant** is a national beauty competition organized by the Miss America Corporation, which awards scholarships for college and graduate school to US women between the ages of 17 to 24.

Modernity is a period marked by a questioning or rejection of traditions, feudalism, and religion and their replacement by scientific, rational, and liberal political ideology and capitalism.

Modernization refers to a model of a progressive transition from a 'pre-modern' or 'traditional' to a 'modern' society.

Multicultural pluralism is the idea of co-existence of cultural differences of diverse minority groups so that they can participate fully in the dominant society yet maintain their differences. In a pluralist culture, minority cultures are not expected to merge into the dominant culture but maintain their cultural differences. See pluralism.

Multinational corporations are international business organizations that may be registered in their home country but conduct business in several countries. They are a form of transnationalism in that they seek to maximize their profits by organizing their operations in locations with the fewest regulations and lowest business taxes, exploiting other countries' natural resources, tax, and cheap labor.

Nationalism is a political ideology that promotes sentiments of loyalty, pride, and devotion to a nation.

National publics refers to groups of people within a nation united by common interests and ideas. In the context of beauty, people within a nation are brought together to watch beauty pageants and discuss and interact with news of them.

Nation-building is the creation of a politically stable, socially cohesive national community through identification with symbols and stories. It can involve mass education, government programs, wars, and propganda.

Neoliberalism is the political and economic theory that individual liberty can best be achieved by reducing state and government interventions in people's lives. Neoliberal policies promote free markets, privatization of public infrastructure, and a reduction of social-welfare programs. See Economic liberalization, Governmental neoliberalism, Liberalism.

Neoliberal self-governance is an identity technique in which market rationales are embodied by self-regulating and self-responsible subjects. It refers to Foucault's idea of cultural power relations that combines free-market rationality and "self-management." See Governmental neoliberalism.

The **New Left**, including the 1960s anti-war student protest movements, the Free Speech Movement, and the hippie movement, broke away from the Old Left, which focused primarily on class and labor issues. In contrast, the New Left broadened its activism to include feminist, anti-racism, and ecological issues.

Normalization refers to social processes through which ideas and actions come to be seen as "normal" and taken for granted in everyday life. Individuals are often rewarded or punished for conforming to or deviating from the ideal of a cultural norm.

A **not-for-profit corporation** is any legal entity organized for general public benefit rather than the interest of its members. It does not make profits for its owners, but is run by like-minded citizens exclusively for social, educational, recreational, or charitable purposes.

Orientalism, or **Orientalist institutionalized white supremacy**. Orientalism is an intellectual tradition that uses cultural representations to highlight an us-and-them binary between the "Occident" and the "Orient" in terms of the superiority of colonial rulers, the Occident, and the inferiority of the colonized, the Orient. The idea is derived from Edward Said's (1978) canonical text, *Orientalism*, which challenged the knowledge-production system by European thinkers and philosophers influenced by colonial structures. The power of such cultural knowledge allowed Europeans to rename, redefine, and thereby control Oriental peoples, places, and things, as imperial colonies.

Overseas Chinese are the transnational population of Chinese migrants whose business and professional achievements have increased China's economic growth.

The **Pan-African Congress** was an anti-colonial organization of Africans set up in 1900 in London that aimed to decolonize Africa and the Third World from European colonization. It focused on black self-determination by connecting with an African diaspora.

Patriarchal ideology is the justification for a social system in which family systems or entire societies are organized around the idea of male power and women are subordinated and largely excluded from it.

Pluralism is acceptance of and respect for different religious, ethnic, racial, and political groups. See Multicultural pluralism.

A **positive-discrimination quota system** is the provision of special opportunities in employment, training, etc., for a disadvantaged group, such as women or ethnic minorities. The US equivalent is the affirmative-action policy.

Postcolonial identity refers to subjectivities created in relation to colonialism either by rejecting or integrating it.

Postcolonialism is the historical phase after colonialism. It is also the study of legacies of nations emerging out of colonialism and grappling with the challenges of self-determination, not least how they incorporate or reject the colonizers' Western norms and conventions.

Postfeminism is understood as a new generation of women's reaction to second-wave feminism. It also describes a backlash against second-wave feminism in media and consumer culture and implies that feminism is finished because women in the West can access education and employment and have therefore achieved equality. In media and consumer culture it is associated with "empowering" and the "individual choice" of women to enjoy their beauty, femininity, and sexuality; but the diffuse power of heterosexual male control is concealed.

Post-structuralism is an academic theoretical framework and an intellectual move- ment that began in France in the 1950s and 60s. It studies the underlying structures in cultural products (such as texts) and uses analytical concepts from linguistics, psychology, anthropology, and other fields to interpret those structures. It has exposed the assumptions of many Western norms.

The **public sphere** is an area of social life where individuals can come together to freely discuss and identify societal problems, and through that discussion influence political action. This idea was developed by German philosopher Jürgen Habermas.

The **Quit India Movement** was a mass non-violent civil-disobedience movement. It was launched in India in August 1942 in response to Mohandas Karamchand Gandhi's call for British withdrawal from India. Until 1945 tens of thousands of Indian freedom activists and leaders were arrested and imprisoned.

Racial assimilation refers to the merging of cultures of racial minorities due to pressure of adaption and for class mobility into majority culture.

Racial capital is Margaret Hunter's term (2005) for a "resource drawn from the body that can be related to skin tone, facial features, body shape, etc."

Racial passing describes assimilation of a person of mixed-race into the white majority to avoid penalties.

Radical feminism is a type of feminism that challenges male supremacy in the patriarchal system of power that organizes society and oppresses women.

Rashtriya Swayamsevak Sangh (RSS) is a right-wing Hindu-extremist paramilitary organization that has organized violence against Christians and Muslims.

The **Reconstruction Era** (1865–77) was a radical period for the history of civil-rights progress in the US in which the eleven Confederate states that had seceded from the Union were restored to it. Laws were brought in giving equal rights to freedmen, and black communities gained power by setting up schools, voting, and winning political office. However, there was a white backlash against black communities' progress, and the Ku Klux Klan terrorized blacks.

Rhinoplasty is plastic surgery performed on the nose.

Roosevelt's The New Deal was a series of programs in response to the Great Depression enacted in the US between 1933 and 1938 by President Franklin D. Roosevelt.

Scientific racism is the use of scientific evidence to support the belief in racism, racial inferiority, or racial superiority.

Second-wave feminism. See Feminism, Second-wave.

Sectarianism is an ideology based on bigotry, discrimination, or hatred arising from perceived differences between religions, classes, regions, or factions of a political movement.

Sizism is fat stigma is closely associated with perceptions of laziness and a lack of self-control or discipline.

Skin-color prejudice/discrimination/colorism is discrimination based on skin color. Colorism is a form of prejudice or discrimination in which human beings are treated differently based on the social meanings attached to skin color. This form of prejudice often results in reduced opportunities for those who are discriminated against on the basis of skin color.

Socialism espouses common or public ownership. Socialism is a social and economic system characterized by social ownership of the means of production and co-operative management of the economy. Socialists believe in creating an equal society that does not rely on making profit out of the labor of the masses.

Socialist feminism describes a mix of two ideologies to achieve women's equality. It does not only focus on gender but on class and overall power relations in a society.

Soft power Soft power is a concept developed by Joseph Nye on how countries use culture, political values, and foreign policies to persuade other countries of their high status.

Soviet-style five-year socialist economic plans were a series of nationwide centralized economic plans based on those of the Soviet Union (USSR) and adopted by most other communist states, including the People's Republic of China and India.

Special Economic Zones (SEZ) are specified areas within a country that have different regulations from other areas, including tax incentives and lower tariffs, to attract foreign direct investment.

Structural assimilation is a term proposed by Milton Gordon, a US sociologist, to explain the different stages of adaptions that minority immigrant communities pass through to attain economic stability and cultural understanding.

Symbolic power refers to cultural power one can mobilize as a resource, such as one's education or one's cultural knowledge.

Third-wave feminism. See Feminism, Third-wave.

Third World feminism refers to a type of feminism that challenges Western feminism's understanding of the universal category of "woman."

Third World women are women from countries of the South.

Third World women's anti-colonial movements refer to feminist social movements influenced by revolutions all around the world against European colonialism. The Third World Women's Alliance (TWWA) was founded in 1971, and, under the leadership of founding member Frances Beale, aimed at unmasking the relation between sexual oppression, racism, and financial exploitation. Its main focus was to unite women of color across anti-imperialist, anti-sexist, and anti-racist political lines.

Township and Village Enterprises (TVE) are geographical areas in China that, in order to attract investment by foreign companies, do not have to adhere to state rules on workers' rights, the minimum wage, and other benefits.

Transnational consumer culture is a culture that crosses borders and relies on construction of cultural symbols and rituals as mediated through global and transnational markets. It is a system in which consumption of commercial products dominates everyday practices.

Transnational cultural flows are the movement of culture, people, ideas, commodities, and finance across national borders, facilitated by global capitalism.

Transnational feminism is an interdisciplinary feminist approach to analyzing gender as an intersectional formation produced by social, political, and economic conditions of nationalism, colonialism, capitalism, and imperialism.

Transnationalism is a social formation of interconnectivity between people across national borders formed as a result of capitalist globalization.

Transnational public sphere. See Public sphere and Transnationalism.

White privilege is a term coined by Peggy McIntosh to refer to unearned benefits and advantages awarded to/accrued by white people due to their economic, cultural, and political dominance. This is not available to non-white people. White people can assume their experiences, ideas, and values are normal and universal and that others' are abnormal and particular.

White-savior narratives are stories in which white men and women get to be heroes and sheroes and rescue people of color from their suffering and oppression. Third World women, men, and minorities are often victims who are dependent on white heroes to end their own oppression.

White supremacy is the belief that white people are superior to those of all other races, especially the black race, and should therefore dominate society. It refers to the systematic institutionalization of the superiority of white races and the justification of Anglo dominance in multiple institutions.

The **Women's Liberation Movement** was a type of radical feminism that began in the 1960s, in the US, with groups such as New York Radical Women (1967–9), and lasted until the end of the 1970s.

The **World Bank** is an international economic organization that provides finance, advice, and research to developing nations to help their economic stability and development.

Bibliography

Adams, N. 2001. Analysis: Nose Jobs in Iran are Becoming More Popular as the Dress Code Allows Women to Leave Only Their Faces Uncovered. NPR, All Things Considered. www.highbeam.com/doc/1P1-46670572.html. Accessed June 18, 2014.

Ahmed-Ghosh, H. 2003. Writing the Nation on the Beauty Queen's Body: Implications for a "Hindu" Nation. Meridians: Feminism, Race, Transnationalism, 4(1): 205–27.

Aldridge, D. 2005. From Civil Rights to Hip Hop: Toward a Nexus of Ideas. The Journal of African American History, 90(3): 226–52.

All-China Women's Federation. 2003. Zhang Xiaomei: Economist in the Beauty Industry. May 8. www.womenofchina.cn/Profiles/Businesswomen/200358.jsp. Accessed December 18, 2014.

Ambedkar, D. B. 1917. Castes in India. In Moon (ed.), Writings and Speeches, Vol. 1. Bombay: Department of Education, Government of Maharashtra.

American Society of Plastic Surgeons (ASPS). 2011. 2011 Plastic Surgery Procedural Statistics. www.plasticsurgery.org/Documents/news-resources/statistics/2011-statistics/2011_Stats_Full_Report.pdf. Accessed December 18, 2014.

Appadurai, A. 1990. Disjuncture and Difference in the Global Cultural Economy. Theory, Culture and Society, 7(2): 295–310.

Appadurai, A. 1996. Modernity at Large. Minneapolis: University of Minnesota Press.

Ayyar, V. and Khandare, L. 2013. Mapping Color and Caste Discrimination in Indian Society. In Hall (ed.), The Melanin Millennium: Skin Color as 21st Century International Discourse. Dordrecht, Heidelberg, New York, London: Springer.

Balogun, O. M. 2012. Cultural and Cosmopolitan: Idealized Femininity and Embodied Nationalism in Nigerian Beauty Pageants. Gender and Society, 26: 357–81.

Banet-Weiser, S. 1999. The Most Beautiful Girl in the World: Beauty Pageants and National Identity. Berkeley: University of California Press.

Banks, I. 2000. Hair Matters: Beauty, Power, and Black Women's Consciousness. New York: New York University Press.

Barlow, T. E. 1993. Colonialism's Career in Postwar China Studies. Positions, 1(1), 224–67.

Barlow, T. E. 2004. The Question of Women in Chinese Feminism. Next Wave: New Directions in Women's Studies. Durham, NC: Duke University Press.

Barlow, T., Dong, M. Y., Poiger, U., Ramamurthy, P., Thomas, L. M. and Weinbaum, A. E. (Modern Girl Around the World Research Group). 2005. The Modern Girl Around the World: A Research Agenda and Preliminary Findings. Gender and History, 17: 245–94.

Bartky, S. L. 1990. Femininity and Domination: Studies in the Phenomenology of Oppression. Hove: Thinking Gender Psychology Press.

BBC News. 2003. Chinese Woman Seeks Perfect Beauty. July 24. http://news.bbc.co.uk/1/hi/world/asia-pacific/3093139.stm. Accessed December 12, 2014.

BBC News. 2003. India Debates "Racist" Skin Cream Ads. July 24. http://news.bbc.co.uk/2/hi/south_asia/3089495.stm. Accessed November 14, 2014.

BBC News. 2004. Beauty Pageant: China's "artificial beauty" show. December 12. http://news.bbc.co.uk/go/pr/fr//2/hi/asia-pacific/4090741.stm. Accessed December 20, 2014.

de Beauvoir, S. 1972. The Second Sex. Translated by H. M. Parshley. London: Penguin.

Berlant, L. 2008. The Female Complaint: The Unfinished Business of Sentimentality in American Culture. Durham, NC: Duke University Press.

Bond, S. and Cash, T. 1992. Black Beauty: Skin Color and Body Images among African-American College Women. Journal of Applied Social Psychology, 22(11): 874–88.

Bonilla-Silva, E. 2006. Racism without Racists: Color-blind Racism and the Persistence of Racial Inequality in the United States. Lanham, MD: Rowman and Littlefield.

Bordo, S. 1989. The Body and the Reproduction of Femininity: A Feminist Appropriation of Foucault. In Jaggar and Bordo (eds), Gender/Body/Knowledge: Feminist Reconstructions of Being and Knowing (pp. 13–33). New Brunswick, NJ: Rutgers University Press.

Bordo, S. 2003. Unbearable Weight: Feminism, Western Culture, and the Body. Berkeley: University of California Press.

Brand, P. 2000. Introduction: How Beauty Matters. In Brand (ed.), Beauty Matters (pp. 1–23). Bloomington, IN: Indiana University Press.

Brown n' Proud. 2014. http://www.brownandproud.org. Accessed August 15, 2014.

Brown, W. 2005. Neoliberalism and the End of Liberal Democracy. In Edgework: Critical Essays on Knowledge and Politics (pp. 1–17). Princeton, NJ: Princeton University Press.

Brownell, S. 2005. China Reconstructs: Cosmetic Surgery and Nationalism in the Reform Era. In Alter (ed.), Asian Medicine and Globalization (pp. 132–50). Philadelphia: University of Pennsylvania Press.

Butler, J. 1990. Gender Trouble: Feminism and the Subversion of Identity. London, New York: Routledge.

Butler, J. 1993. Bodies that Matter: On the Discursive Limits of "Sex". London, New York: Routledge.

Cahill, A. J. 2003. Feminist Pleasure and Feminine Beautification. Hypatia, 18(4): 42–64.

de Casanova, E. M. 2004. No Ugly Women: Concepts of Race and Beauty among Adolescent Women in Ecuador. Gender and Society, 18(3): 287–308.

Census of India. 2011. http://censusindia.gov.in/. Accessed June 22, 2014.

Césaire, A. 1972. Discourse on Colonialism. Translated by J. Pinkham. New York: Monthly Review Press.

Chandra, B. 1989. India's Struggle for Independence, 1857–1947. New Delhi: Penguin Books India.

Chong, D. 2014. Collective Action and the Civil Rights Movement. Chicago: University of Chicago Press.

Cohen, B. C., Wilk, R., and Stoeltje, B. 1996. Beauty Queens on the Global Stage: Gender, Contests, and Power. New York: Routledge.

The Combahee River Collective. 2014. www.feministezine.com/feminist/modern/Black-Feminist-Statement. html. Accessed 21 March, 2014.

Cooper, A. J. 1988. A Voice from the South. New York, Oxford: Oxford University Press.

Craig, M. Leeds. 2002. Ain't I a Beauty Queen? Black Women, Beauty, and the Politics of Race. New York: Oxford University Press.

Craig, M. Leeds. 2006. Race, Beauty, and the Tangled Knot of a Guilty Pleasure. Feminist Theory, 7(2): 159–77.

Crenshaw, K. 1991. Mapping the Margins: Intersectionality, Identity Politics, and Violence against Women of Color. Stanford Law Review 43(6): 1241–99.

The Daily Beast. 2013. In China, "Leftover Women" Get Plastic Surgery. 8 April. www.thedailybeast. com/articles/2013/08/04/in-china-leftover-women-get-plastic-surgery.html. Accessed November 25, 2014.

Dargis, M. 2015. Review: What Happened, Miss Simone? New York Times, June 24. www.nytimes. com/2015/06/24/movies/review-what-happened-miss-simone-documents-nina-simones-rise-as-singer-and-activist.html?_r=0. Accessed June 24, 2015.

Davis, A. Y. 1974. An Autobiography. New York: Random House.

Davis, A. Y. 1983. Women, Race and Class. New York: Random House.

Davis, K. 1995. Reshaping the Female Body: The Dilemma of Cosmetic Surgery. New York: Routledge.

Davis, K. 2003. Dubious Equalities and Embodied Differences: Cultural Studies on Cosmetic Surgery. Lanham, MD: Rowman and Littlefield.

Dore, M. 2014. She's Beautiful when She's Angry. New York: International Film Circuit.

Dow, B. 2003. Feminism, Miss America, and Media Mythology. Rhetoric and Public Affairs, 6(1): 127–49.

Du Bois, W. E. B. 1903. The Souls of Black Folk. Chicago: A. C. McClurg and Co.

Du Bois, W. E. B. 1935. Black Reconstruction in America: An Essay toward a History of the Part which Black Folk Played in the Attempt to Reconstruct Democracy, 1860–1880. New York: Harcourt, Brace.

Durham, A. 2007. Using [Living Hip-Hop] Feminism: Redefining an Answer (to) Rap. In Durham, Pough, Raimist and Richardson (eds), Home Girls Make Some Noise: Hip Hop Feminism Anthology (pp. 304–12). Mira Loma, CA: Parker Publishing.

Durham, A. 2012. Check On It: Beyoncé, Southern Booty, and Black Femininities in Music Video. Feminist Media Studies, 12(1): 35–49.

Durham, A., Pough, G., Raimist, R., and Richardson, E. (eds) 2007. Home Girls Make Some Noise: Hip Hop Feminism. Mira Loma, CA: Parker Publishing.

Dutt, B. 2008. We the People. National Development Television.

The Economist. 2004. Business: Saving Face; China's Beauty Business. July 10: 63.

Edmonds, A. 2007. "The Poor Have the Right to be Beautiful": Cosmetic Surgery in Neoliberal Brazil. Journal of the Royal Anthropological Institute, 13(2): 363–81.

Edmonds, A. 2010. Pretty Modern: Beauty, Sex, and Plastic Surgery in Brazil. Durham, NC: Duke University Press.

Eisenstein, Z. R. 1978. The Combahee River Collective. Capitalist Patriarchy and the Case for Socialist Feminism. Boston, MA: South End Press.

Emanuelle, K. 2014. June 30. http://darkisbeautiful.blogspot.in/. Accessed December 18, 2014.

Fan, L. 2011. Last Train Home. Montreal: EyeSteelFilm. http://www.last-train.com/. Accessed July 17, 2014.

Fanon, F. 1967a. Black Skin, White Masks. Translated by C. L. Markmann. New York: Grove Press.

Fanon, F. 1967b. The Wretched of the Earth. New York: Grove Press.

Feldstein, R. 2005. "I Don't Trust You Anymore": Nina Simone, Culture, and Black Activism in the 1960s. The Journal of American History, 91(4): 1349–79.

Fernandes, L. 2000a. Nationalizing "the Global": Media Images, Cultural Politics and the Middle-class in India. Media, Culture and Society, 22(5): 611–28.

Fernandes, L. 2000b. Restructuring the New Middle-class in Liberalizing India. Comparative Studies of South Asia, Africa and the Middle East, 20(1): 88–104.

Fernandes, L. and Heller, P. 2006. Hegemonic Aspirations. Critical Asian Studies, 38(4): 495–522.

Ferrell, C. L. 2006. The Abolitionist Movement. Westport, CT: Greenwood Publishing Group.

Firestone, S. 1970. The Dialectic of Sex: The Case for Feminist Revolution. New York: William Morrow.

Foucault, M. 1982. The Subject and Power. Critical Inquiry 8(4): 777–95.

Foucault, M., Burchell, G., Gordon, C. and Miller, P. 1991. The Foucault Effect: Studies in Governmentality. Chicago: University of Chicago Press.

Fraser, N. 2013. Fortunes of Feminism: From State-managed Capitalism to Neoliberal Crisis. London: Verso Books.

Frey, W. H. 2004. The New Great Migration: Black Americans' Return to the South, 1965–2000. Center of Urban and Metropolitan Policy, the Brookings Institution. www.brookings.edu/research/reports/2004/05/demographics-frey. Accessed August 22, 2014.

Freyre, G. 1956. The Masters and the Slaves: A Study in the Development of Brazilian Civilization. New York: Knopf.

Friedan, B. 1963. The Feminine Mystique. New York: W.W. Norton and Co.

Frisby, C. M. 2004. Does Race Matter? Effects of Idealized Images on African American Women's Perceptions of Body Esteem. Journal of Black Studies, 34(3): 323–47.

Fuss, D. 1989. Essentially Speaking: Feminism, Nature and Difference. New York, London: Routledge.

Gaines, K. 1996. Uplifting the Race: Black Leadership, Politics, and Culture in the Twentieth Century. Chapel Hill: University of North Carolina Press.

Garbus, L. 2015. What Happened, Miss Simone? Los Gatos, CA: Netflix.

Gates, H. L. 2013. The African Americans: Many Rivers to Cross. PBS. www.pbs.org/wnet/african-americans-many-rivers-to-cross/about/about-the-series/. Accessed July 12, 2014.

Gill, R. and Scharff, C. (eds) 2011. New Femininities: Postfeminism, Neoliberalism and Subjectivity. Basingstoke: Palgrave Macmillan.

Gimlin, D. 2000. Beauty as Commodity. Qualitative Sociology, 23(1): 77–98.

Giroux, Henry A. 1994. Disturbing Pleasures: Learning Popular Culture. New York: Routledge.

Glenn, E. Nakano. 2008. Yearning for Lightness: Transnational Circuits in the Marketing and Consumption of Skin Lighteners. Gender and Society, 22(3): 281–302. doi: 10.1177/0891243208316089.

Glenn, E. Nakano (ed.) 2009. Shades of Difference: Why Skin Color Matters. Palo Alto, CA: Stanford University Press.

Godfrey, M. 2004. World 'beauty makers' knocking China door. China Daily, April 6. www.chinadaily.com.cn/english/doc/2004-04/06/content_321064.htm. Accessed December 15, 2014.

Goodman, A. and Gonzalez, J. "I Am Not Nonviolent": New Nina Simone Film Captures Singer and Activist's Uncompromising Voice. www.democracynow.org/2015/6/24/new_nina_simone_documentary_what_happened. Accessed June 28, 2015.

Gordon, M. 1981. America as a Multicultural Society. Philadelphia: American Academy of Political and Social Science.

Grewal, I. 1999. Traveling Barbie: Indian Transnationality and New Consumer Subjects. Positions, 7(3): 799–827.

Grewal, I. 2005. Transnational America: Feminisms, Diasporas, Neoliberalisms. Durham, NC and London: Duke University Press.

Gullickson, A. 2005. The Significance of Color Declines: A Re-Analysis of Skin Tone Differentials in Post-Civil Rights America. Social Forces, 84(1): 157–80.

Gupta, J. 2012. Understanding Colorism. August 3. http://jyotigupta.org/understanding-colorism-an-interview-with-dr-radhika-parameswaran/. Accessed September 18, 2014.

Gupta, R., Sankhe, S., Dobbs, R., Woetzel, J., Madgavkar, A., and Hasyagar, A. 2014. India's Path from Poverty to Empowerment. McKinsey Global Institute Report. www.mckinsey.com/insights/asiapacific/indias_path_from_poverty_to_empowerment. Accessed November 15, 2004.

Habermas, J. 1991. The Structural Transformation of the Public Sphere: An Inquiry into a Category of Bourgeois Society. Cambridge, MA: MIT Press.

Hall, R. E. (ed.) 2013. The Melanin Millennium: Skin Color as 21st Century International Discourse. Dordrecht, Heidelberg, New York, London: Springer.

Hall, S. 1992a. The West and the Rest: Discourse and Power. In Hall and Gieben (eds), Formations of Modernity (pp. 275–320). Cambridge: Polity Press.

Hall, S. 1992b. The Question of Cultural Identity. In Hall, Held, and McGrew (eds), Modernity and Its Futures (pp. 274–316). Cambridge: Polity Press.

Hall, S. 1997. Representation: Cultural Representations and Signifying Practices. London: SAGE Publications.

Hall, S. 2000. Conclusion: The Multi-cultural Question. In Hesse (ed.), Un/settled Multiculturalisms: Diasporas, Entanglements, Transruptions (pp. 209–41). London, New York: Zed Books.

Hall, S. 2001. The Multicultural Question. Milton Keynes: Open University Pavis Centre for Social and Cultural Research, Faculty of Social Sciences.

Hamermesh, D. and Biddle, J. 1994. Beauty and the Labor Market. The American Economic Review, 84(5): 1174–94.

Hanisch, C. 1970. The Personal is Political. In Firestone and Koedt (eds), Notes from the Second Year: Women's Liberation. Major Writings of the Radical Feminists (pp. 76–8). New York: Radical Feminism. http://www.carolhanisch.org/CHwritings/PIP.html. Accessed July, 2014.

Hanisch, C. 2014. Carol Hanisch of the Women's Liberation Movement. www.redstockings.org/. Accessed July 2014.

Harris, C. 1995. Whiteness as Property. In Crenshaw (ed.) Critical Race Theory: The Key Writings that Formed the Movement (pp. 276–91). New York: The New Press.

Harvey, D. 2007. A Brief History of Neoliberalism. Oxford: Oxford University Press.

Harvey, L. and Gill, R. 2011. Spicing It Up: Sexual Entrepreneurs and the Sex Inspectors. In Gill and Scharff (eds), New Femininities: Postfeminism, Neoliberalism and Subjectivity (pp. 52–67). Basingstoke: Palgrave Macmillan.

Herring, C. 2003. Skin Deep: How Race and Complexion Matter in the "Color-Blind" Era. Illinois: University of Illinois Press.

Hill, M. E. 2002. Skin Color and the Perception of Attractiveness among African Americans: Does Gender Make a Difference? Social Psychology Quarterly, 65(1): 77–91.

Hill-Collins, P. 1990. Defining Black Feminist Thought. In Black Feminist Thought: Knowledge, Consciousness, and the Politics of Empowerment. New York: Routledge.

Hill-Collins, P. 2006. From Black Power to Hip Hop: Racism, Nationalism, and Feminism. Philadelphia: Temple University Press.

Hill-Collins, P. 2009. Emerging Intersections: Building Knowledge and Transforming Institutions. In Dill and Zambrana (eds), Emerging Intersections: Race, Class, and Gender in Theory, Policy, and Practice (pp. vii–xv). New Brunswick, NJ: Rutgers University Press.

hooks, b. 1989. Black Beauty and Black Power: Internalized Racism. Boston, MA: South End Press.

hooks, b. 1992. Black Looks: Race and Representation. Toronto: Between the Lines.

hooks, b. 1996. Killing Rage: Ending Racism. New York: St Martin's Press.

hooks, b. 2000. Feminist Theory: From Margin to Center. London: Pluto Press.

hooks, b. 2005. Black Women Shaping Feminist Theory. Cambridge: ProQuest Information and Learning.

hooks, b., Mock, J. and Blackman, M. 2014. Are You Still a Slave? Liberating the Black Female Body. www.youtube.com/watch?v=rJk0hNROvzs. Accessed July 25, 2014.

Hull, G. T., Scott, P. B. and Smith, B. (eds) 1981. All the Women Are White, All the Blacks Are Men, But Some of Us Are Brave: Black Women's Studies. Old Westbury, NY: Feminist Press.

Hunter, M. L. 2002. "If You're Light You're Alright": Light Skin Color as Social Capital for Women of Color. Gender and Society, 16(2): 175–93.

Hunter, M. L. 2005. Race, Gender, and the Politics of Skin Tone. New York: Routledge.

Hunter, M. L. 2011. Buying Racial Capital: Skin Bleaching and Cosmetic Surgery in a Globalized World. Journal of Pan African Studies, 4(4): 142–64.

Hutchinson, G. 1997. The Harlem Renaissance in Black and White. New York: Belknap Press.

Inniss, L. and Feagin, J. R. 1989. The Black "Underclass" Ideology in Race Relations Analysis. Social Justice, 16(4): 13–34.

International Monetary Fund. 2015. World Economic Outlook (WEO) Update, July. www.imf.org/external/pubs/ft/weo/2015/update/02/index.htm. Accessed July 27, 2015.

Jacques, M. 2012. China: The Beginning of a New World Order. The New Statesman, April 18. www.newstatesman.com/economics/economics/2012/04/beginning-new-world-order. Accessed July 25, 2014.

Jayawardena, K. 1986. Feminism and Nationalism in the Third World. Delhi: Kali for Women.

Jeffreys, S. 2005. Beauty and Misogyny: Harmful Cultural Practices in the West. London: Routledge.

Jha, M. R. 2006. The Emotional Politics of Bombay Cinema and the British Asian Imaginary. Doctoral dissertation, Goldsmiths College, University of London.

Jha, M. R. 2007. The Politics of Emotion in British Asian Experiences of Bombay Cinema. Journal of Creative Communications, 2(1–2): 101–21.

Jodhka, S. S. and Prakash, A. 2011. The Indian Middle Class: Emerging Cultures of Politics and Economics. KAS International Reports. www.kas.de/wf/doc/kas_29624-544-2-30.pdf. Accessed September 15, 2014.

Jones, G. 2008. Blonde and Blue-Eyed? Globalizing Beauty, c.1945–c.1980. The Economic History Review, 61(1): 125–54.

Joseph, P. E. 2006. The Black Power Movement: Rethinking the Civil Rights–Black Power Era. Abingdon, New York: Routledge.

Kang, L. 2004. Globalization and Cultural Trends in China. Honolulu: University of Hawaii Press.

Kaplan, C. and Grewal, I. 1994. Transnational Feminist Cultural Studies: Beyond the Marxism/Poststructuralism/Feminism Divides. Positions: East Asia Cultures Critique, 2(2): 430–45.

Karnani, A. 2007. Doing Well by Doing Good Case Study: "Fair & Lovely" Whitening Cream. Stephen M. Ross School of Business at the University of Michigan, Ross School of Business Working Paper Series No. 1063.

Kaw, E. 1993. Medicalization of Racial Features: Asian American Women and Cosmetic Surgery. Medical Anthropology Quarterly, 7(1): 74–89.

Kaw, E. 1994. Opening Faces: The Politics of Cosmetic Surgery and Asian American Women. In Sault (ed.), Many Mirrors: Body Image and Social Relations (pp. 241–65). New Brunswick, NJ: Rutgers University Press.

Keith, V. M. and Herring, C. 1991. Skin Tone and Stratification in the Black Community. American Journal of Sociology, 97: 760–78.

Kelley, R. 2002. Freedom Dreams: The Black Radical Imagination. Boston, MA: Beacon Press.

Knowles, B. 2005. Check On It (music video). Sony, US.

Kreydatus, B. 2008. Confronting the "Bra Burners": Teaching Radical Feminism with a Case Study. The History Teacher, 41(4): 489–504.

Kumari, J. 1986. Feminism and Nationalism in the Third World. New Delhi: Kali for Women.

Kwan, S. and Fackler, J. 2008. Women and Size Factsheet. Sociologists for Women in Society (SWS), Network News 25(1): 38–45.

Kwan, Samantha. 2009. Framing the Fat Body: Contested Meanings Between Government, Activists, and Industry. Sociological Inquiry 79(1): 25–50.

Kymlicka, W. 1995. Multicultural Citizenship: A Liberal Theory of Minority Rights. Oxford: Clarendon Press.

Lauretis, T. de. 1991. Queer Theory: Lesbian and Gay Sexualities. An Introduction. Differences: A Journal of Feminist Cultural Studies, 3(2): iii–xviii.

Lavender, C. 2009. The Cult of Domesticity and True Womanhood. City University of New York. http://www.library.csi.cuny.edu/dept/history/lavender/386/truewoman.html. Accessed July 15, 2014.

Lee, S. H. 2012. The Geopolitics of Beauty: Race, Transnationalism, and Neoliberalism in South Korean Beauty Culture. Unpublished doctoral dissertation.

Lemann, N. 1986. The Origins of the Underclass: Part I. The Atlantic, 257(6): 31–55.

Levine, L. W. 1978. Black Culture and Black Consciousness: Afro-American Folk Thought from Slavery to Freedom. Oxford: Oxford University Press.

Lewis, D. L. (ed.) 1995. The Portable Harlem Renaissance Reader. New York: Penguin Group USA.

Li, H. 2013. TCM in Skin Whitening and Lightening: The Eternal Pursuit in East Asia. GCI Magazine, April 4. www.gcimagazine.com/marketstrends/regions/bric/TCM-in-Skin-Whitening-and-Lightening-The-Eternal-Pursuit-in-East-Asia-201466981.html. Accessed December 18, 2014.

Li and Fung Research Center. (2011). China's Cosmetic Market. www.idsgroup.com/profile/pdf/industry_series/Issue17_Cosmetics.pdf. Accessed April 2011.

Liu, L. 2013. Chinese Feminism: The Birth of Chinese Feminism. In Liu, Karl and Ko (eds), Essential Texts in Transnational Theory. New York: Columbia Press.

Loong-Yu, A. and Shan, N. 2007. Chinese Women Migrants and the Social Apartheid. Development, 50(3): 76–82.

Lury, C. 1996. Consumer Culture. Cambridge: Polity Press.

McIntosh, P. 2015. White Privilege: Unpacking the Invisible Knapsack. In Andersen and Hill-Collins (eds), Race, Class, and Gender (pp. 74–9). London: Cengage Learning.

McRobbie, A. 2004. Post-feminism and Popular Culture. Feminist Media Studies, 4(3): 255–64.

McRobbie, A. 2009. The Aftermath of Feminism: Gender, Culture and Social Change. London: SAGE.

Mazumdar, S. 1989. Race and Racism: South Asians in the United States. Pullman, WA: Washington State University Press.

Mire, A. 2005. Pigmentation and Empire: The Emerging Skin-whitening Industry. July 28. www.counterpunch.org/mire07282005.html. Accessed March 2014.

Miss America Organization. www.missamerica.org/default.aspx. Accessed February 20, 2014.

Moallem, M., Kaplan, C. and Alarcon, N. (eds) 1999. Between Woman and Nation: Nationalisms, Transnational Feminisms, and the State. Durham, NC: Duke University Press.

Mohanty, C. T. 1991. Under Western Eyes: Feminist Scholarship and Colonial Discourses. In Mohanty, Russo and Torres (eds), Third World Women and the Politics of Feminism. Indianapolis: Indiana University Press.

Mohanty, C. T. 2003. Feminism without Borders: Decolonizing Theory, Practicing Solidarity. Durham, NC: Duke University Press.

Moraga, C. 1983. Loving in the War Years/lo que nunca paso por sus labios. Boston, MA: South End Press.

Moraga, C. and Anzaldúa, G. 1981. This Bridge Called My Back: Writings by Radical Women of Color. San Francisco: Aunt Lute Press.

Moreno Figueroa, M. G. and Rivers-Moore, M. 2013. Introduction: Beauty, Race and Feminist Theory in Latin America and the Caribbean. Feminist Theory, 14(2): 131–6.

Morgan, J. 1999. When Chickenheads Come to Roost: A Hip-hop Feminist Breaks It Down. New York: Simon and Schuster.

Morgan, R. 1968. No More Miss America. www.redstockings.org/index.php?option=com_content&view=article&id=65&Itemid=103. Accessed August 24, 2014.

Morgan, R. 1970. Sisterhood is Powerful: An Anthology of Writings from the Women's Liberation Movement. London: Random House.

Morrison, T. 1970. The Bluest Eye. New York: Washington Square Press.

Moynihan, D. P. 1965. The Negro Family: The Case for National Action. Office of Policy Planning and Research, US Department of Labor.

Munshi, S. 1998. Wife/Mother/Daughter-in-law: Multiple Avatars of Homemaker in 1990s Indian Advertising. Media, Culture and Society, 20(4): 573–91.

National Campaign on Dalit Human Rights. www.ncdhr.org.in/ndmj. Accessed September 12, 2014.

Nguyen, M. T. 2011. The Biopower of Beauty: Humanitarian Imperialisms and Global Feminisms in the War on Terror. Signs: Journal of Women in Culture and Society, 26(2): 359–83.

Noble, D. 2000. Ragga Music: Dis/Respecting Black Women and Dis/reputable Sexualities. In Hesse (ed.), Un/settled Multiculturalisms: Diasporas, Entanglements, Transruptions (pp. 148–69). London, New York: Zed Books.

Nye, J. 2005. Soft Power: The Means to Success in World Politics. New York: Public Affairs, US.

O'Neill, J. 2001. Building Better Global Economic BRICs. Goldman Sachs Global Economics Paper No. 66. www.goldmansachs.com/our-thinking/archive/archive-pdfs/build-better-brics.pdf. Accessed September 15, 2014.

Ong, A. 1999. Flexible Citizenship: The Cultural Logics of Transnationality. Durham, NC: Duke University Press.

Ong, A. 2006. Neoliberalism as Exception: Mutations in Citizenship and Sovereignty. Durham, NC: Duke University Press.

Ong, A. 2010. Spirits of Resistance and Capitalist Discipline: Factory Women in Malaysia. Albany, NY: Suny Press.

Ong, A. and Nonini, D. M. (eds) 1999. Ungrounded Empires: The Cultural Politics of Modern Chinese Transnationalism. London and New York: Routledge.

Osuri, G. 2008. Ash-coloured Whiteness: The Transfiguration of Aishwarya Rai. South Asian Popular Culture, 6: 109–23.

Oza, R. 2001. Showcasing India: Gender, Geography, and Globalization. Signs: Journal of Women in Culture and Society, 26(4): 1067–95.

Pahuja, N. 2010. The World Before Her. West Hollywood, CA: Storyline Entertainment.

Parameswaran, R. 2001. Global Media Events in India: Contests over Beauty, Gender, and Nation. Journalism and Communication Monographs, 3(2): 52–105.

Parameswaran, R. 2004. Spectacles of Gender and Globalization: Mapping Miss World's Media Event Space in the News. Communication Review, 7(4): 371–406.

Parameswaran, R. 2005. Global Beauty Queens in Post-liberalization India. Peace Review, 17(4): 419–26. www.tandfonline.com/loi/cper20. Accessed January 30, 2014.

Parameswaran, R. and Cardoza, K. 2007. Fairness/Lightness/Whiteness in Advertising: The Mobility of Beauty in Globalizing India. Paper presented at the meeting of the International Communication Association.

Parameswaran, R. and Cardoza, K. 2009. Melanin on the Margins: Advertising and the Cultural Politics of Fair/Light/White beauty in India. Journalism and Communication Monographs, 11(3): 213–74.

Parekh, B. 2000a. The Future of Multi-ethnic Britain. London: Profile Books.

Parekh, B. 2000b. Rethinking Multiculturalism: Cultural Diversity and Political Theory. London: Macmillan.

Park, R. 1939. Race Relations and the Race Problem. Durham, NC: Duke University Press.

Peoples, W. A. 2008. Under Construction: Identifying Foundations of Hip-Hop Feminism and Exploring Bridges between Black Second-wave and Hip-Hop Feminisms. Meridians: Feminism, Race, Transnationalism, 8(1): 19–52.

Perry, I. 2006. Buying White Beauty. Cardozo Journal of Law and Gender, 12: 579–607.

Philips, A. 2004. Gendering Colour: Identity, Femininity and Marriage in Kerala. Anthropologica, 46(2): 253–72.

Phillips, L., Reddick-Morgan, K. and Stephens, D. P. 2005. Oppositional Consciousness within an Oppositional Realm: The Case of Feminism and Womanism in Rap and Hip-Hop, 1976–2004. The Journal of African American History, 90(3): 253–77.

Pough, G. 2004. Check It While I Wreck It: Black Womanhood, Hip-Hop Culture, and the Public Sphere. Boston, MA: Northeastern University Press.

Rajagopal, A. 1998. Advertising, Politics and the Sentimental Education of the Indian Consumer. Visual Anthropology Review, 14: 14–31.

Rajesh, M. 2013. An Unfair Obsession with Lighter Skin. The Guardian, August 14.

Rangappa, A. 2013. Miss America and the Indian Beauty Myth. The Huffington Post, September 17. www.huffingtonpost.com/asha-rangappa/miss-america-and-the-indian-beauty-myth_b_3941524.html. Accessed March 20, 2014.

Reddy, D. 2005. Caste as Ethnicity. Anthropological Quarterly, 78(3): 543–84.

Reddy, V. 2011. Jhumpa Lahiri's Feminist Cosmopolitics and the Transnational Beauty Assemblage. Meridians, 11(2): 29.

Reddy, V. 2013. Jhumpa Lahiri's Feminist Cosmopolitics and the Transnational Beauty assemblage. Meridians: Feminism, Race, Transnationalism, 11(2): 29–59.

Rondilla, J. L. and Spickard, P. 2007. Is Lighter Better? Skin-tone Discrimination among Asian Americans. Lanham, Boulder, New York, Plymouth: Rowman and Littlefield.

Rose, N. 1988. Inventing Our Selves: Psychology, Power and Personhood. Cambridge: Cambridge University Press.

Rose, N. 1990. Governing the Soul: The Shaping of the Private Self. London, New York: Routledge.

Rose, T. 1994. Black Noise: Rap Music and Black Culture in Contemporary America. Middletown, CT: Wesleyan University Press.

Rottenberg, C. 2014. The Rise of Neoliberal Feminism. Cultural Studies, 28(3): 418–37.

Runkle, S. 2004. Making Miss India: Constructing Gender, Power and the Nation. South Asian Popular Culture, 2: 145–59. doi: 10.1080/1474668042000275725.

Russell, K., Wilson, M. and Hall, R. 1992. The Color Complex: The Politics of Skin Color among African Americans. San Diego, New York: Harcourt Brace Jovanovich.

Russell-Cole, K., Wilson, M. and Hall, R. 2013. The Color Complex: The Politics of Skin Color in a New Millennium. New York: Anchor Books.

Said, E. 1978. Orientalism: Western Representations of the Orient. New York: Pantheon.

Said, E. W. 1993. Culture and Imperialism. New York: Knopf.

Sandberg, S. 2013. Lean In: Women, Work, and the Will to Lead. London: Random House.

Sandoval, C. 1991. US Third World Feminism: The Theory and Method of Oppositional Consciousness in the Postmodern World. Genders, 10: 1–24.

Sandoval, C. 2000. Methodology of the Oppressed. The University of Minnesota Press: Minneapolis.

Scharff, C. 2014. Gender and Neoliberalism: Exploring the Exclusions and Contours of Neoliberal Subjectivities. Theory, Culture, and Society blog. http://theoryculturesociety.org/christina-scharff-on-gender-and-neoliberalism/. Accessed June 18, 2015.

Schein, L. 1994. The Consumption of Color and the Politics of White Skin in Post-Mao China. Social Text, (41): 141–64.

Schiller, H. I. 1976. Communication and Cultural Domination. New York: International Arts and Sciences Press.

Scott, D. M. 2012. How Black Nationalism Became Sui Generis. The Association for the Study of African American Life and History, 1(2): 6–63.

Sedgwick, E. K. 1993. Epistemology of the Closet. In Abelove, Barale, and Halperin (eds), The Lesbian and Gay Studies Reader (pp. 45–61). New York and London: Routledge.

Sekayi, D. 2003. Aesthetic Resistance to Commercial Influences: The Impact of the Eurocentric Beauty Standard on Black College Women. The Journal of Negro Education, 72(4): 467–77.

Shah, A. 2010. www.globalissues.org/article/4/poverty-around-the-world#WorldBanksPovertyEste. Accessed December 16, 2014.

Simmons, R. G. 1978. Blacks and High Self-esteem: A puzzle. Social Psychology, 41: 54–7.

Simon, B. 2006. The World's Most Beautiful Woman? CBS News. 31 Oct. www.cbsnews.com/stories/2004/12/29/60minutes/printable663862.shtml. Accessed February 28, 2014.

Simone, N. and Cleary, S. 2003. I Put a Spell on You: The Autobiography of Nina Simone. Boston, MA: Da Capo Press.

Slater, D. 1997. Consumer Culture and Modernity. Cambridge: Polity Press.

Slaughter, A. 2012. Why Women Still Can't Have It All. The Atlantic Magazine. www.theatlantic.com/magazine/archive/2012/07/why-women-still-cant-have-it-all/309020/. Accessed July 16, 2014.

Smith, A. 2010. Nationalism. Key Concepts in Social Science Series. Cambridge: Polity Press.

Spender, D. 1983. There's Always Been a Women's Movement This Century. London: Pandora.

Spickard, P. 2007. Almost All Aliens: Immigration, Race, and Colonialism in American History and Identity. New York and London: Routledge.

Steger, M. 2013. Globalization: A Very Short Introduction. Oxford: Oxford University Press.

Surinder, S. J. and Prakash, A. 2011. The Indian Middle Class: Emerging Cultures of Politics and Economics. Kas International Reports, 12.

Tate, S. 2007. Black Beauty: Shade, Hair and Anti-Racist Aesthetics. Ethnic and Racial Studies, 30(2): 300–19.

Thapar, R. 1990. A History of India. London: Penguin.

Thompson, C. 2009. Black Women, Beauty, and Hair as a Matter of Being. Women's Studies: An inter-disciplinary Journal, 38(8): 831–56.

Tomlinson, J. 1999. Globalization and Culture. Chicago: University of Chicago Press.

Turner, F. J. 1920. The Significance of the Frontier in American History. In The Frontier in American History. New York: Henry Holt and Company.

UN CERD: Committee On the Elimination of Racial Discrimination. 2007. 17th session, February 9–19 March.

UN Development Institute. www.in.undp.org/content/india/en/home/ourwork/povertyreduction/overview.html. Accessed September 15, 2014.

UN Development Programs. www.in.undp.org/content/india/en/home/countryinfo/. Accessed October 22, 2014.

UN Works. 2012. End Poverty: MDGs 2015. www.un.org/works/sub2.asp?lang=en&s=17. Accessed November 28, 2012.

Van Deburg, W. L. 1992. New Day in Babylon: The Black Power Movement and American Culture, 1965–1975. Chicago: University of Chicago Press.

Wade, P. 1997. Race and Ethnicity in Latin America. London: Pluto Press.

Wen, H. 2013. Buying Beauty: Cosmetic Surgery in China. Hong Kong: Hong Kong University Press.

White, R. T. 2013. Missy "Misdemeanor" Elliott and Nicki Minaj: Fashionistin' Black Female Sexuality in Hip-Hop Culture—Girl Power or Overpowered? Journal of Black Studies, 44(6): 607–26.

Wilson, W. J. 1984. The Black Underclass. The Wilson Quarterly, 8: 88–99.

Winddance Twine, F. 1998. Racism in a Racial Democracy: The Maintenance of White Supremacy in Brazil. New Brunswick, NJ: Rutgers University Press.

Wolf, N. 1991. The Beauty Myth: How Images of Beauty Are Used against Women. New York: William Morrow and Company.

Women of China. 2007. Miss World 2007 Wants to Help People in Need. December 4. www. womenofchina.cn/womenofchina/html1/people/others/8/9256-1.htm. Accessed December 12, 2014.

Women of China. 2012. China's Plastic Surgery Craze. March 21. www.womenofchina.cn/. Accessed November 28, 2012.

World Bank. 2012. Inequality in Focus, 1(1). http://siteresources.worldbank.org/EXTPOVERTY/Resources/Inequality_in_Focus_April2012.pdf. Accessed November 27, 2012.

World Bank. Data: GDP Growth (Annual %). http://data.worldbank.org/indicator/NY.GDP.MKTP.KD.ZG. Accessed December 16, 2014.

X, Malcolm. 1964. The Autobiography of Malcolm X. London: Penguin.

Xu, G. and Feiner, S. 2007. Meinü Jingji/China's Beauty Economy: Buying Looks, Shifting Value, and Changing Place. Feminist Economics, 13(3/4): 307–23.

Yang, J. 2011. Nennu and Shunu: Gender, Body Politics, and the Beauty Economy in China. Signs: Journal of Women in Culture and Society, 36(2): 333–57.

Zacharias, U. 2003. The Smile of Mona Lisa: Postcolonial Desires, Nationalist Families, and the Birth of Consumer Television in India. Critical Studies in Media Communication, 20(4):388–406.

Index

abolitionist movement 36
ACWF *see* All-China Women's Federation
Adivasis tribal groups 58
African Americans *see* Black is Beautiful
Afro Pride 40–2
ageism 83–5
Ahmed-Ghosh, H. 62–3
Aldridge, D. 40
All the Women Are White, All the Blacks Are Men, But Some of Us Are Brave (Hull *et al.*) 20
All China Women's Federation (ACWF) 82–3, 85, 86
alternative modernity in China 77
Ambedkar, B. R. 58–9
American exceptionalism myth 28
Anglo-conformity 25–9
Anglo-European beauty norms *see* white ideology
anti-black racism 25–6
anti-colonial movements 20, 57–8
anti-colorism campaigns 68–71
anti-racist beauty aesthetics 31–51
anti-war demonstrations 14–15
Anzaldúa, G. E. 20
Are You Still a Slave: Liberating the Black Female Body? online panel discussion 45–6
Aryan race theory 66, *see also* racism
Asian model minority myth 28
assimilation 36–7, 57

Ayyar, V. 65–6

Bandung Conference 38
Banks, I. 40–1
Barlow, T. 79, 86
Beauty Beyond Color campaign 68–9
beauty contests/pageants 13–14, 24–5, 28–9, 41, 60–3, 81–2
beauty justice campaigns 68–71
Beauvoir, S. de 17–18
Bei, W. 83
Beyoncé 45–50
Bharatiya Janata Party (BJP) 59
Biddle, J. 24
BJP *see* Bharatiya Janata Party
black feminism 19–20, 39
Black is Beautiful 31–51; Beyoncé 45–50; history 35–40; hypersexuality 48–9; impact on identity 40–2; light-skin privilege 44–5; positive body self-esteem 43–4; racial capital 47–8; self-hatred 43–4; sexual empowerment 48–9
Black Panther Party 39
Black Power movement 20, 36–7, 39
Black Skin, White Masks (Fanon) 38–9
Blackman, M. 45–6
blepharoplasty 84
Bollywood 26, 27, 68–9
Bond, S. 43

internalized colorism 67–8
International Monetary Fund (IMF) 59
International Society of Aesthetic Plastic Surgery (ISAPS) 81–2
Internet 81–2, *see also* social media
intersectionality 19–20

Jacques, M. 79
Jain, C. 70–1
Jayawardena, K. 55
Jim Crow laws 37–8

K-wave culture (Korean wave) 79
Kang, L. 78–9
Karnani, A. 68
Kelley, R. 37, 39
Khan, S. R. 69
Khandare, L. 65–6
King, M. L. 26
Korea 82, *see also* K-wave culture
Kwan, S. 22–3

Lauretis, T. de 20
Lean In (Sandberg) 49
"leftover women" 83–4
Li, H. 87
liberal feminism 16, 17–18
liberal multiculturalism 28
light-skin privilege 44–5, *see also* colorism
liposuction 84
Liu, L. 86
L'Oreal cosmetics 63–4
loss, cultural 57
lynching 37–8

McRobbie, A. 23
Malcolm X 36
male-dominated business sectors 85
Mandal Commission 58–9
march for racial/economic equality 19
Marxist feminism 15–16, 18–19
Mao Tse-tung *see* Zedong, M.

media consumer culture 21–2
media moral panics 28
medicine 87
meinu jinji (beauty pageants) 82
military 60–1
Mistry, A. 64
Mock, J. 45–6
Mohanty, C. T. 55
Moraga, C. 20
moral panics 28
Morrison, T. 44
Moynihan, D. 43
MTV 45–7
multicultural diversity 25–9
multicultural mobility 63–4
Munshi, S. 61
music 40, 45–7, 48–50
Muslim women 23

National Organization for Women (NOW) 16
nationalism 13–30; Black is Beautiful 35–40; China 81–2; Indian 52–72
nativism 57
Negritude 38
Negro Improvement Association (UNIA) 38
Nehru, J. 58
nennu to shunu 83–4
neoliberalism 13–30, 49–50; Black is Beautiful 49–50; China 79–83; Indian nationalism 63–4
new sexism 21–4
New York march for racial/economic equality 19
New York Radical Women (NYRW) 14–16
newspapers 82
Ngozi, C. 45
Noble, D. 48
not-for-profit corporations 13, 14, 24–5, 28–9
NOW *see* National Organization for Women
NYRW *see* New York Radical Women

Ong, A. 80–1
online panel discussions 45–6